The Corbin Story

A Memoir

IDEAS & RISK - A LIFE OF INVENTION

The Corbin Story

————————————— *A Memoir* —————————————

ONE MAN'S LIFETIME OF IDEAS & RISK - A LIFE OF INVENTION

The Authorized Biography

by
William Graham Carrington

A Pennyworth Book

Published June, 2005

Corbin (first edition)
Copyright © 2005 by William G. Carrington.

Excerpts from this book have appeared in or as articles in a number of regional and national magazines and newsletters.

Cover Concept - Mike Corbin
Cover Art - Joni Montag
Editing by Donna D. Karakash
Final edit by William Carrington
Graphics and Type - Michelle Jenkins

Library of Congress Catalog Card Number: 2005904191
Carrington, William G. , 1945-
      Corbin

ISBN   978-1-888701-36-4
ISBN   1-888701-36-6 (paper)

Copies of this book may be obtained from Pennyworth Press, POB 25176, Asheville, NC 28813.
Electronic orders and information requests should be directed to
books@pennyworthpress.com - On The World Wide Web -
        http://www.pennyworthpress.com
Copies are also available from Corbin Saddles - Hollister, CA / Daytona, FL

This book is dedicated to those who ride and enjoy the unique brotherhood we are all able to participate in because of motorcycles - and especially those of us who are able to go a few extra comfortable miles because of a Corbin saddle.

Acknowledgements

I would like to thank those people without whose assistance this book would have never been possible. First of all my editorial and graphics support staff Donna D. Karakash, Michelle Jenkins, and Pete Savage for the moral support, long hours, and patience with a short tempered biker / author on way too little sleep.

Jean Lara of Corbin-Gentry whose historical data proved invaluable in piecing together the early years. Likewise, Al Simmons of Mustang Motorcycle Seats, for additional background and identifying segments of time at Corbin-Gentry.

The staff at Corbin Pacific for their help and patience, especially Greg and Joni in marketing. To Sandy, Mike's right arm, who's had more to do for me in the months leading up to this book than she has Mike. Tom Corbin, Vince the Wiz, Chance, Cher, and Julio for their input.

Ben Franklin, in Poor Richard's Almanac said, "Fish and Guests stink in three days". I have to thank Bev Corbin for allowing me to stay in their home many times, for much longer than it takes fish or guests to go long past stinking. Last, but certainly not least, my deepest gratitude to Mike Corbin, my friend for over a decade. For the friendship, hospitality, and generosity, and for patiently putting up with endless hours of questions and taping by me for the research for this book.

Thank you all, and Mike - Thank you my friend.

Foreword

I first met Mike Corbin in the early 1970's in my official capacity as a State inspector at his Somersville, Connecticut plant. Typical of Mike, he had saved an old woolen mill and turned it into an environmentally responsible manufacturing plant. Mike recognized my passion for building custom motorcycles and we soon became close friends. I had already owned two semi-stock Harleys and used one of Mike's hardtail extended frames and custom seats to construct my first "chopper". Subsequently, Mike and I designed and built prototype frames for Harley powered trikes (for our three wheeled motorcycle enthusiasts) and café style racers. These prototypes were then used to construct jigs on which production frames we manufactured for sale to the custom bike market. Mike became consumed by the need to encourage motorists to demand and purchase environmentally sound technology. His practical knowledge of electricity and electromotive force led him on a quest to dispel a prevailing myth concerning the use of electric vehicles, that they were slow. He assembled a team from among his company employees and some of his friends, like me, who believed in Mike and wanted to contribute to his vision and set out to break the land speed record for an electric vehicle. The rest is history.

Mike has been a visionary, entrepreneur, team builder, problem solver, scientist, engineer and inventor all of his life. He has managed to accomplish these feats with a grace and style, which is unique and unspoiled by "conventional learning and belief". With all of the accolades, which can be heaped upon Mike, perhaps the most important is his humanity, which he has always displayed to his employees, colleagues and friends. Mike is a true one of a kind "idea man" and I am fortunate to be considered one of his friends.

Anthony V. Sadinas

Mr. Sadinas has an undergraduate degree from the University of Connecticut in the sciences. He holds one masters degree from the University of Hartford and performed his masters and doctoral work at Yale University with an emphasis in administration. Mr. Sardinas is currently a Senior Vice President and Commercial Director at Wall Street Systems in New York.

Preface

This is an American story. An all American story. A story of one man who liked to build things. An inventor, a maker of widgets, an experimenter who was interested in understanding the workings of existing things, and finding ways of making them work better. Among his keenest areas of interest were aerodynamics of motion and electricity.

This could be a story about one of America's colonial inventors. Easily Thomas Jefferson and his machines, or perhaps Benjamin Franklin, who's kite flying pioneered experimentation with electricity. Neither of these, however, are the subjects of this story,

nor is it the genius of steam transportation, Robert Fulton. Even though our subject bears a passing resemblance to Ben Franklin, this story is a 20th century tale.

The subject of the story is the son of Irish Immigrants who grew up instilled with an Irish work ethic, and an insatiable curiosity about what makes things tick. Additionally he was possessed with a passionate interest in harnessing electromotive force.

His description could fit the Wright Brothers or either of the inventive cohorts Thomas Alva Edison and Henry Ford. After all, Henry Ford was the son of Irish immigrant parents and made widgets, and had a keen interest in both transportation and electricity.

The widget-maker in this American story was born in New England in 1943, midway through the Great War.

Twenty-five years later, our second-generation Irish experimenter has served a hitch in the Navy, and is employed as an electrician at a major manufacturing company.

By the year 1968 the United States was in the midst of another devastating war. The economy was on the eve of destruction, and the populace was unknowingly soon to become disillusioned with the government and the blind faith belief in the infallibility of an ideology it had been taught since the beginning of the baby boom generation.

1968 also saw the fulfillment of an old cliché, which states that, "necessity is the mother of invention." In this case the necessity was a need to travel more comfortably and led to the invention of a device to do just that. For the creation of a single seat to improve the ride on a Norton motorcycle led to an empire of invention and manufacturing in the motorcycle industry, and all under the name Corbin.

By the close of the 20th century, the Corbin logo was second only to Harley-Davidson as a recognized brand marque to the world of American-made two-wheeled transportation. As the single most desirable add-on accessory in the industry, fully one third of the new motorcycles sold in America annually were re-fitted with Corbin Saddles.

The early interest in electricity coupled with a love of motorcycles led to electric motorcycles and during the oil embargo of the mid 70s, development of replacement electric engines for VWs.

Corbin, at one time, held the land speed records for both two and four-wheeled vehicles powered by electricity. The two-wheeled record still stands unbroken.

The success of the seat business facilitated a resurrection of his interest in electrically powered transport, and gave birth to the development of the ill-fated Sparrow.

The Sparrow was a three-wheeled all electric car which was licensed as a motorcycle. This vehicle, like Henry Ford's electric car a century earlier, succumbed to the lack of current technology's ability to efficiently supply power for the engine. This is not a new problem. In the 19th Century repeating rifles and Babbage's first computer suffered from the lack of contemporary technology sufficient to supply necessary materials.

The ingenuity and success of Corbin's endeavors caught the interest of the Harvard School of

Business, which elected to pursue an in-depth and comprehensive study into the phenomenon, and the lessons to be learned, and taught to America's rising entrepreneurs and business executives.

This candid and intimate look into the world of Corbin isn't merely a history of the man, the seats, the bikes, and the cars. While it is all that, it is also a look into the how and why of the successes, and the failures, as Mike Corbin shares the story of his life and business. This book also explains to the would-be entrepreneur how Mike went through the re-invention of himself and the business, repeatedly, in order to achieve success. In doing so the book teaches the reader how to achieve a similar success in the motorcycle industry. Its lessons provide a road map for the newcomer to achieve that goal.

An entrepreneur, hungry for success and intelligent enough to learn from the lessons taught here, might well apply them to achieve success in any business endeavor.

So I invite you, the reader, to settle back, relax, and in the following pages, learn how one man began with a single item thirty-eight years ago and achieved the American Dream.

CONTENTS

Chapter One
The Early Years 2

Chapter Two
The School Years 10

Chapter Three
Wheels, Water, and Electricity 21

Chapter Four
War, Peace, and Nowhere to Sit 32

Chapter Five
Corbin Gentry 46

Chapter Six
Making Sparks Fly 67

Chapter Seven
Changes in Attitudes Changes in Longitutes 98

Chapter Eight
Reinventing Corbin 111

Chapter Nine
From Castroville to Dreams Fulfilled 145

Chapter Ten
Fly Sparrow Fly 163

What's special about Mike Corbin is that he came along and, of all the people in the United States, Mike Corbin was the only one that made 300 Sparrows. Nobody else even tried, but he did it. So, it didn't quite make it. The fact that he tried is important. I lost some money in it, and I don't regret it in any way. It was the right thing to do. It's too bad it didn't come out.

-Charlie MacArthur

Corbin's Ride On *- The planets aligned and the networks agreed to take the show and Mike seized the moment. He is brilliant and he is so visionary. Not everything he touches turns to gold, but he is not afraid to take risks. You will fail sometimes when you do that, but you will never fly if you fear risks...and Mike soars.*

-Dennis Gage - Producer - Corbin's Ride On, My Classic Car

Mike Corbin - Visionary

Chapter 1
The Early Years

Beginning with the potato famine, a great influx of Irish emigrants had begun in the United States. While a few had been here since colonial times, nothing was to match the masses that came here during the mid 19th century. While the Irish were to be found within all segments of the US, most of these emigrants settled in the New England regions, providing a glut of available and cheap labor. Many present day historians argue that the influx of cheap Irish labor was a contributing factor among the events that led to the American Civil War. The Irish work ethic was to become high among the virtues linked to the American identity.

By the 1940s, the United States was in the midst of a great war that for the most part, had enveloped the whole world. Midway through this conflict, a relatively typical Irish emigrant couple from Gardner, Massachusetts, gave birth to a son. Born November 3, 1943, Mike Corbin was the first of three children born to Walt and Mary. Christened Michael Walter, he would precede the birth of his brother Stephen Gregory, by two years, and an unnamed sister who was stillborn by four.

Mike's family was not atypical. As an emigrant couple both parents worked hard but provided a relatively normal life for themselves and their children, at least for the times and area. Mike recalls that his childhood was uncomplicated. They didn't have much, but there was always good food on the table and he never lacked for clean clothes.

Mike's father, Walt, was a tool and die maker for the furniture industry and Mary worked as a secretary.

Mary was an extraordinary typist and exhibited a mastery of word skills. During her career, she worked for several companies. She was possessed of the Irish competitive nature, entering numerous typing contests, and winning many of them.

His father worked in the furniture industry for several companies over time as a career toolmaker and upholsterer. This provided Mike an early influence in the area of mechanical skills that would come to serve him well.

Another influence in Mike's early development was his uncle, Dan, Mary's older brother. Dan was a self-employed mechanical engineer with a degree from Brown University. Dan had never married and spent a lot of time with Mike and his parents. Uncle Dan owned a franchise repairing AMF bowling pinsetters. He also had a line of pinball machines placed in various cafes, bars, and diners which were routinely serviced. Walt and Mike worked for Dan off and on and according to Mike, his dad and uncle could fix anything.

Dan's primary income came from being a mechanical engineering consultant for the furniture industry, which involved setting up and servicing the automatic equipment that cut out mass-produced chair parts. The town of Gardner was known at the time as the chair capitol of the world. These machines, called cam shapers, were the predecessors of modern computerized (CNC) fabricating machines.

As a kid working for Uncle Dan and Walt, Mike was in and out of many shops running tools and working as a helper. This experience gave him lots of good exposure to machinery and he learned much about how things worked.

In addition to everything else, Dan was an excellent gunsmith, and Mike spent many hours learning a fair amount about the workings of small items and went hunting and fishing often with his father and uncle. Dan was a lifelong bachelor who took care of Mike's grandmother until his death at a fairly early age from diabetes.

A story, which emphasizes Mike's early ability with gadgets, as well as his father's wisdom and sense of humor, happened about age six or seven. Mike had taken his dad's alarm clock apart and was learning how it worked when his Uncle Bill came over to visit. Bill was a rough and red-faced Irishman with a brusque personality and a

Mike & Stevie - '48

drinking problem. He noticed that Mike had the clock apart and suggested that Walt reprimand the boy severely for dismantling the clock and slap him around a bit to teach him a good lesson. Walt replied, with a touch of humor in his voice, that maybe they ought to wait until he had put the clock back together before they slapped him around.

In 1953, a tragic event occurred, which was to affect the whole family, and inadvertently start the youngster on a path of reinvention. This was the death of Mike's younger brother, Stephen, when Mike was ten. Stephen, familiarly known as Stevie,

Mike & Stevie - '51

was at the playground with his father and fell from a swing tripod about 14 feet high. The fall resulted in a very bad fracture of his left arm. A major surgical procedure was required to repair the fracture, including the installation of two metal plates in his forearm to hold the bones together. This surgery was successful but left him with a large raised area where the plates were attached. Once the bones had healed additional surgery was necessary to remove the plates. This surgery had tragic results. The ether used for anesthesia had somehow become poisoned. Stephen passed away due to the toxic ether. Another child was poisoned at that same time from the bad ether. This tragedy caused irreparable damage to Mike's family.

Stephen had been terrified of the follow up operation and feared that it would take his life and said as much to his mother. He told her, "Well I'll never see you again, I love you — goodbye — cause I probably won't make it through the operation." Mary, while taking his fear seriously, also believed it was only the child's fear of the surgery causing him to speak this way. Stephen and the

6

other child (a little girl) died in the surgery the next day.

In addition to the heartbreak from the death of Stephen, both of Mike's parents were ridden with unwarranted guilt - Walt for being at the playground with him and not being able to prevent the accident, and Mary from her son's statement prior to the surgery and having not stopped the procedure. Mary had already been seriously affected emotionally by the loss of her daughter six years earlier and this compounded the emotional state brought on by Stephen's death.

Mike and Stevie - 1950

Only the onset of Alzheimer's late in life would bring relief from her emotional state.

Between the two of them, they both persecuted themselves the remainder of their lives. They became somewhat withdrawn and spent most of their time immersed in their respective jobs, leaving Mike to pretty much depart from a typical childhood, reinvent, and raise himself.

Mike developed a passionate interest in models, particularly those electric ones with remote controls, such as electric boats, planes, and rockets. Walt and Mary, while if not openly supportive, never tried to stop these interests.

When Mike was ten years old, he was in a Boy Scout Troop for a short time. An unfortunate incident brought this avocation to an untimely end. One snowy night on a camping trip, the Scout Master crawled into the tent with Mike and another boy and snuggled between the two and offered them cigarettes. The boys went home and told their parents. Mike's dad was understandably furious and scouting was ended for Mike.

Throughout these early years, Mike was raised as an only child and looked more and more inward to himself for direction and personal growth. He had an ever-growing disappointment with family finances and stature and some resentment toward his parents. He was bordering on being disappointed in them for what he perceived as a lack of success and accomplishment. An attitude which today, in retrospect, he understands was not the case at all and speaks of them with pride in their own accomplishments and success in life by rising above the depths of poverty as simple emigrants.

Mike's father insisted upon a strict work ethic and demanded that Mike earn any major item he acquired. One such item was a bike he had his heart set to own.

Mike saw one of the first three-speed Raleigh bicycles in a shop window and was enraptured over the prospect of having a bike like that. Mike was about eight years old and these bikes had just hit the market. Although he had a bike given to him earlier by his parents, this one was special. Mike rushed home to convince his dad to buy him that bike. The chosen approach was to present his pitch to his dad from a need standpoint. He told him that he really needed that bicycle and Walt walked along with him in a fatherly stance and listened as Mike presented his case. He needed that bicycle and with it he could carry papers and earn the money to pay his dad back for buying him the bike. When Mike finished his argument, his dad told him, "Son, you don't need a bicycle, what you need is a job."

His dad made him get the job and earn the money to buy the Raleigh three-speed. A lesson Mike never forgot. Mike relates, to this very day that, that incident affected him to the extent that today he has a whole collection of motorcycles numbering in the thirties.

Chapter 2
The School Years

High school was, at best, a paradox in Mike Corbin's life. On one hand, here is a guy who has an insatiable appetite for exploring and learning, while at the same time having no appetite for books and academics. This is still a strange paradox since the Mike Corbin of today is a Harvard Business School alumni, a voracious reader, and a collector of books.

In actuality, the high school years found Mike's involvement with models and making things turning to more complex projects and more original widgets, models, and contraptions. He hated homework, but he loved working alone at home and where his academics suffered, he did, however, make great models.

The four years spent in high school were at best an emotional roller coaster. He was divided between the personal rewards of successfully crafting various ideas into realities and having to endure an ever-widening gulf of boredom as a trade-off. A few of the projects helped bridge the gap, however, and one was actually a bridge itself. With the growing problems in school hitting him face on, came the added negativity at home with the communication gap between himself and his parents. Walt and Mary, like virtually all parents, wanted their son to "make something of himself." Also, like almost all parents, they thought they knew best what he should do to achieve this end and like most children Mike had different ideas.

An additional problem was that he was going to Notre Dame, a Catholic high school, for the first three years. This was a problem in as much as it was steeped in tradition and church related discipline, while the son of Walt and Mary was anything but traditional and disciplined in directions of that nature.

Mike would spend countless hours educating his mind in the directions he wished to head and almost no time doing the tried and true methods that required studies prescribed by the teachers at school. He stayed in trouble for not doing his homework, which created not only a conflict between Mike and the school, but also revolved back onto his home life with reports from the teachers to his parents. These reports, in turn, rolled over onto Mike with reprimands and disciplinary actions taken by his parents who seemed to be perpetually upset with him.

Mike found it very hard to pay attention in class. He felt that he wasn't being taught what he wanted to learn and always stayed in trouble for not participating and not doing his homework. He remembers that most of his time in school was spent watching the activities of the pigeons on the school ledges rather than listening to the teachers. In spite of this lack of interest in school and effort, he managed to get by with Bs and B+s anyway, which wasn't too bad, considering.

The situation was further compounded by the tendency of some of the Jesuit brothers to "goose" Mike and a few other students. Those students, who were the unlucky recipients of this unwanted attention, would suddenly find, while on the stairs or a crowded hallway, what was termed at the time, "having a snake in your pants."

Those few brothers who practiced these activities quickly figured out which kids had parents who wouldn't believe it if they were reported and persecuted them while leaving others alone. A few incidents such as this, and an unhappy experience as an alter boy, turned Mike against the school and the church itself.

Perhaps in the far-reaching grand view, looking back, this situation provided some of the fuel for Mike's departure from conventional thought and made him look beyond the box. Questioning the establishment in his young mind, he saw that things were not as they were presented, and this frustration forced him to go within his own mind to find solutions and direction. All of his quality time was spent working on his projects in his small basement shop at home. He would go there right after school and then back after supper to work and experiment until bedtime making models, radio gear, and other electronic stuff.

One bright spot was there in spite of the communications gap between Mike and his father. His dad was able to understand the love of building things and began to bring home gears and random parts for Mike to tinker with in his various home projects.

Mike's parents were among those who had absolute faith in the church and had worked hard to provide the resources to send Mike to this school, which was also a relatively long commute from his home. The school was about 20 miles away and required taking a school bus to and from school until Mike was old enough to drive his own car. They attributed the problems with Mike to his being a nonconformist. A role he saw himself in as well and embraced. He was an avid fan of the

TV show, Dobie Gillis, and completely identified with the Maynard G. Krebbs character, even to the attitude, speech, and expressions. His teachers got really angry when Mike called them "Teach" instead of Brother So-and-So.

High school, according to Mike, was spent suffering the continuously widening gap between him and his parents and marking time until he could get through four years to graduation and either join the Navy or hop a freight train.

Some things, however, salved the problems and made it easier to get through the process. Among these were the projects, which brought a great sense of pride and satisfaction to the disgruntled teenager.

Perhaps, his only interest in high school academics was science, and he was a member of the physics and science clubs. Mr. Beaudoin, the physics teacher, was his favorite and Mike recalls that this was the only teacher to whom he ever listened.

His love of making things led to the construction of a working drawbridge, which he entered in the annual science fair and won First Grant. This was the term used to designate a first place award.

Inspired by this ray of hope, in an otherwise bleak outlook, he undertook a seriously huge project in his second year.

Mike began to build a working robot, which stood 4' 2" high and rolled under its own power on rigid legs crafted from a Sears fiberglass kit. The torso was shaped from clear Plexiglas to make the insides visible. The arms worked and used a magnet for one hand and a claw contraption as the other. Most of the parts and wiring were obtained from Uncle Dan and were gleaned from discarded bowling alley equipment. Servomotors operated the arms and drive wheels while a stepping relay for an AMF pinsetter machine was the head and brain. Mike worked out memory circuits so that it could do repetitive actions. The robot was nicknamed Robbie by Mike's friends from the movie *Forbidden Planet*. Robbie won the science fair First Grant in Mike's second year of high school. With continuous upgrades and improvements, Robbie won the third year Grant as well.

Ultimately, the problems with the Jesuit brothers caused Mike to quit Notre Dame High and, much to his parent's dismay, transfer to public high school in his hometown of Gardner, Massachusetts.

Gardner High was not a significant development in Mike's life, but it did provide a greater level of freedom and even more determination to join the Navy.

Robbie posing beside Mike's awards.

Mike's tinkering and learning did not stop with robots and things done in the small basement shop. Bigger projects were tackled as well.

About 1959, his mother had bought a 1957 Plymouth and gave Mike her old 1951 Plymouth. Getting this car on the road was Mike's first big project and was his transportation from his junior year in school through graduation.

Like most kids of his day, he began immediately to customize it by removing the chrome and filling the holes. Walt laughingly said, "It looked like the car had the measles."

Mike's propensity to get in trouble and be able to escape by the skin of his teeth reared its head right away with the car. He was not old enough to drive when he first got the car and would sneak it out when his parents weren't at home and go for long drives along the beautiful country roads of New England.

After Mike began driving on a regular basis, he was caught driving under the influence. The policeman, however, had been a school friend of Mike's mother, so rather than giving Mike a ticket, he reported Mike to his mother instead. This incident was repeated a couple of more times while he owned the Plymouth. Mike had the luck of the Irish with him even then because he was never arrested, nor was his license ever revoked.

Lessons that were to be learned in repairing automotive sized equipment began with replacing a blown rear crankshaft seal and bearings in the car. Eventually a cracked head had to be replaced as well.

The beginnings of a lifelong involvement with motorcycles began around this period with the purchase, behind his parents' backs, of a Lambretta motor scooter.

It seems that Mike had a best friend, who was the Gardner, Massachusetts's equivalent of *Leave It To Beaver*'s Eddie Haskell. Ernie was his name and he was the "maximum ultra nonconformist." Mike's parents strongly disapproved of the friendship, but Ernie was his friend and had a Vespa scooter himself and along with another friend also named Mike, helped him cover up the bike purchase. It came to Mike with a price tag of

$25.00 and wasn't running. Mike hid it at Ernie's house and worked on it until he got it running again and would ride it in secret. Secret, that is, until he crashed it and had to go home with his trousers torn and a portion of his skin left on the road. This accident made the discovery of the scooter's existence by Walt and Mary inevitable.

With the secret out in the open finally, Mike brought the scooter home and was able to keep it in the basement and maintain it there.

Prior to the Lambretta, a seed had already been planted in Mike's psyche. Mike had ten uncles in his family. Five were paternal and five were maternal and he was close to about five or six of them, collectively, who were into motorcycles. Springfield and Gardner, Mass. are adjacent cities and Indian Motorcycles was located in Springfield. Several of Mike's uncles had worked at the plant during WW II and this gave Mike exposure to the world of motorcycles at a very early age. The desire to have one and ride was an understandable natural inclination.

There were no more robots or bridge projects in the fourth and last year of school. Mike had made a deal with his parents to be able to join the Navy. He had made two attempts to run away from home so they agreed that if he would graduate first, then they would sign for his under age enlistment. He wanted nothing more than to get away from Gardner and the life he had known, to go out and see the world.

For his senior year, Mike spent his time, for the most part, hanging out with his girlfriend and other friends and just making plans for joining the Navy.

The favorite pastime for Mike and his friends was to spend afternoons after school and weekends driving over to the Triumph motorcycle shop in Townsend, Mass. named The Little Green Triumph Shop; this was a magic place for the teens to congregate. In addition to the motorcycles, the shop owner had "dirty magazines" for the guys to look at. This would-be rowdy bunch could ride over there, drink cokes, look at the risqué pictures, and sit on the bikes and dream of being in the wind. They all wanted to be like Johnny in the movie *The Wild One.*

His dad had told him, however, there were three things he could not do. One was to smoke cigarettes, and two was drink, and the third was that he couldn't go see that movie *The Wild One.* To defy such an edict Mike stole cigarettes from his dad and used the money to buy a bottle of beer and go to the theater and watch *The Wild One.*

Eventually, school's end and graduation arrived bringing the cool times to an end and the prospects of a life radically changed from anything Mike had ever known. He was off to see the world.

Chapter 3
Wheels, Water, and Electricity

Although he did not consciously think of it as such at the time, Mike was undergoing the first reinvention of himself as a person and that person's direction in life. Walt and Mary had originally had their hearts set on Mike attending a more traditional formal education. Because of the science fairs and grades, he could have attended Worcester Polytechnic Institute in nearby Worcester, Mass. By this time, the communication gap between Mike and his parents had developed almost into an adversarial relationship and attempts at conversation always seemed to end up in an argument. In addition, since attending Worcester Tech would have meant still living at home, Mike held his ground and after the conclusion of Mike's high school career, his parents kept their word and signed for his enlistment in the Navy.

He would later attend Worcester Tech as an

outside part time student for some coursework, but for the present, he was going to get his formal training in the Navy, get as far away from Gardner as possible, and get to see the world.

Mike sold his car and then reported for duty at the US Navy boot camp at the Recruit Training Command in Great Lakes, Illinois.

While at recruit training, Mike became deeper in his involvement with motorcycles. A friend had a 1959 Triumph Bonneville for sale and Mike wanted it bad enough to buy it even though he couldn't ride it right away. The asking price was $1000.00 and Mike had only $300.00 in cash of his own. He negotiated the price down to $800.00 and talked his dad into a loan for the rest. Walt made the loan somewhat grudgingly and said he would never do it again. The bike was delivered to his parents' house and stored in the basement to await Mike's return. Mike was able to ride it when home on leave and did so in uniform.

Mike did well in boot camp. After a few days to get over the shock and into the training program attitude, he settled in to doing his best. He was very much aware that in order to get his preferred schooling in either electronics or electrician training he would have to do well. He qualified for both and chose the shorter of the two and decided on Electrician's Mate School.

Upon completing basic training, he took leave back in Gardner and then returned to Great Lakes where the school was located. He proved to be a good student, made great grades, and the result was that he was allowed first choice in selecting his duty location. In as much as his goal was to get as far from Gardner as possible, he chose the USS Ranger. The CVA-61 Ranger was an Aircraft Carrier based in the San Francisco Bay area. San Francisco had a distant romantic ring to Mike.

Mike arrived early and went straight to the docks to see the ship. He remembers being in awe of such a huge vessel and how majestic an aircraft carrier could be. He was totally thrilled that he was going to be an electrician on board this carrier.

He had shipped his sea bag out there by Greyhound Bus and rode the Triumph across the country, carrying only the barest necessities and an army sleeping bag. The trip was not without some minor repairs on the bike, but went fairly uneventfully.

As soon as he saw the Ranger at the dock, he made up his mind to be the best electrician on board. This decision was one he was to keep and put into practice. He made sure he was the most squared away guy and no matter what needed to be repaired, Mike's response was to say, "Yes sir

I'll fix it right away." True to his legacy as a child with the alarm clock story, he loved learning about everything and making it work. He loved fixing anything and making it work better. This is an attitude he still has and applies to the design of seats and other part improvements for motorcycles.

Mike made arrangements for a safe place to keep the Triumph and reported for duty aboard the Ranger.

Once on board the ship and having reported for duty, he was asked by a chief electrician, "What makes you think you can come all the way out here from A School and be an electrician? What makes you think you can fix anything?" The Chief was apparently reacting to Mike's confident and brassy attitude. Mike said, "Well Chief, I rode a Triumph motorcycle all the way out here from Massachusetts." To which the Chief replied, "I think you'll do all right."

Mike's enlistment was a great experience and he loved his hitch in the Navy. He found everything in the service that he never found in high school. He even considered staying in as a career choice and planned for his life to go in that direction.

While in the service, he matured as a person. The Navy was his first real successful educational structure, and it could be said that he grew up on board ship. He could have gone to Officers Candidate School just as he had earlier had the opportunity to go to college, but chose not to do so. Nevertheless, he dedicated himself to being the perfect enlisted man. His journeymanship on the ship went well and he found it easy to work with others who had more seniority. He seemed to excel at finding his way around and honed the skill of figuring things out. He never got in trouble, was never disrespectful, always paid attention to the job at hand, passed every test, and was always recommended for advancement by his superiors. Mike achieved the maximum grade level in his enlistment.

He did everything he was asked, including climbing masts, although that was not a part of his job. The feeling of self-esteem grew constantly greater with the ever-widening knowledge that he could learn and fix everything on board the ship. In fact, he loved fixing everything no matter the piece of equipment. From main generators to flight deck lighting, he would happily work on it, and as an E-5 electrician, was one of the first call when a problem arose. Mike laughingly says, "It makes you the first one dragged out of bed at night when there is a problem."

His strongest talent seemed to be troubleshooting. There is a huge urgency on board a ship when equipment fails, and a rush to find out "why is it broken, where is it broken, and how fast can we fix it." This knack of being able to ascertain what is wrong with a piece of equipment and correcting it would serve him well later in his career outside of the Navy. This unique ability was hinted at as a child and was evidenced in the incident with the alarm clock.

Mike in the Navy - 1962

He loved being on board ship so much that sometimes on warm nights he would go topside and lie in the nets placed around the sides of the flight deck to catch things that rolled or slid off the flight deck. He would just lie in the net and enjoy looking out at the ocean flowing by the ship. The beautiful South Pacific nights were simply an awesome place to contemplate the world.

Mike met his first wife because he was in the Navy. A close friend and fellow ship's electrician, Fred Gerard, invited him to a party. It was expected that the party would be attended by a number of his shipmate's former classmates.

He met Susan Lee at the party and they began to date and were soon married. It was a simple wedding with no family in attendance. The distance and his father's health prevented Walt and Mary from traveling to California.

Mike and Susan were married in the summer of 1964. Not long after, with Susan expecting their first child, Mike was honorably discharged from the Navy at Treasure Island. The marriage and pregnancy did not precipitate the discharge, but rather the declining health of Mike's father became the deciding factor. Walt had developed lung cancer.

Mike actually had a job after his discharge arranged in San Francisco. The arrangement was that upon being discharged, he would begin work at the shipyard as an electrical draftsman.

He loved the west coast, and had spent his leave time in the Bay area motorcycling around the hills and frequenting the watering holes haunted by other motorcyclists. He admired their free spirited lifestyle and loved nothing better than the sense of adventure and freedom that only a motorcycle could provide.

When the Ranger was docked at Alameda Naval Air Station Mike would go into Oakland and loved watching the Hells Angels and their chopper Harleys. Mike found inspiration in their freedom and silently admired Sonny Barger.

This was the era when clubs like the Hells Angels were just beginning to get a lot of attention and notoriety from state officials and the local law as well. It was 1964 that politicians really discovered that bike clubs, which shocked polite society, made a good drum to beat for political platform fodder. This political weapon was to backfire over time, for instead of putting an end to them, America embraced the image of freedom, and the expansion of such clubs spread across the country exponentially.

As exciting as life was for Mike, his deep involvement in such a life and the industry it was incubating would have to wait a few more years in as much as life as he had come to know it once again going to change drastically.

With a first child on the way, it was decided that Walt should get to know his grandchild before his passing. Mike and Susan found themselves driving across the United States for a return to Gardner and the start of a new life together.

The following five years found Mike doing well as an electrician back in New England. The couple's first son, Thomas Walter, was born in the spring of 1965, and three more children would be born to Mike and Susan. They are in order of appearance, a daughter Kelly in 1967, Michael Timothy in 1968, and another daughter, Erin, in 1970.

It wasn't too hard for Mike to find work back in Massachusetts. The paper mill, in nearby Fitchburg, needed electricians and were only too happy to hire a Navy trained manipulator of wires to service the electronics that made the machinery function. Mike held this job for about a year and a half.

Walt and grandson Tom

Better working conditions and better pay led to seeking work across state lines in Connecticut.

Connecticut had a lot of defense contractors building the war machinery to support our military efforts in Viet Nam. One of these giant contractors was Pratt & Whitney in East Hartford.

Mike and Susan moved with the job to Connecticut and he became a heavy machinery mover for Pratt & Whitney. That is, he was the person who moved the electrical controls and reset them up on the machine when one of the massive Vertical Turret Lathes had to be installed or relocated. These are the lathes used to machine the turbine rings for jet engines, and Pratt was the chief supplier of jet engines to the Viet Nam war effort.

Living so close made it easy for Mike and Sue to travel back and forth to Gardner to visit the ailing Walt, and alternately Mary would often bring Walt to Connecticut for visits.

Walt passed away in 1967 from the cancer. He had been born in 1898 and was 69 years old.

By 1970, Mike and Sue's marriage was in trouble, and by 1972, they were divorced. Sue moved back to California taking the kids with her. Mike and his kids visited back and forth on a regular basis as they grew up. Mike traveled to California 3 or 4 times a year to see them, and the kids came east in the summers. Mike took the kids on trips overseas whenever possible. The demise of his marriage was a surprising turn in the life of this electrician who first wanted to stay in the Navy and live in San Francisco.

Mike's first big surprise when he returned from the Navy was to discover that everything was cleaned out of his basement shop and the robot had been thrown in the dump. This would not be the only shocking change to affect his life back in New England and elsewhere. The evolution of reinventing Mike Corbin was only beginning.

Chapter 4
War, Peace, and Nowhere to Sit

Mike's life had taken a sudden turn with the move to Connecticut. The work was good and steady as long as there was a war going on. Mike had worked for other companies for a while, but no place longer than six months to a year. He was just not happy working for someone else.

Mike in Connecticut, after returning from the Navy

He had been doing well at Pratt & Whitney and as the war heated up the demand increased for jet engines. More and more independent contractor shops were taking on the machining of jet engine parts. The demand for the type of electrical installation had widened considerably. With Pratt & Whitney farming out machine work to subcontractors, they had to send out their own workers to move these machines around and set up the electronics.

The demand was so great that in 1966, Mike decided to strike out on his own and form a small electromechanical contracting business to subcontract his labor and fill the demand. He acquired his own crew and supplied the skilled labor to move and hook up the machines that Pratt & Whitney was locating in the independent shops. The setup involved locating, leveling, balancing and wiring them, and there were more machines being setup than there was labor, so Mike's small company stayed busy. According to Mike, the phone was ringing off the hook.

This was Mike Corbin's first business venture on his own, and it was successful. He was making more money than he had ever made as an employee anywhere.

Soon he had two trucks, another master electrician, and two helpers. With two crews and all of the defense suppliers, Mike was, "busier than a one armed paper hanger."

The area manufacturing was primarily based around aircraft and guns. Predominant were companies supplying the aircraft industry like Pratt & Whitney, Sikorsky, and Hamilton, while the major gun makers were also there. Names such a Colt, Savage, Winchester, and Marlin were prominent.

Mike, in addition to installing the VTLs, had outside contracts with Colt Firearms and the now defunct Loring Laboratories.

Opening this business was a fortuitous decision for Mike because it eventually led him back to building things rather than fixing things. However, the things he builds are in a way designed to fix something.

The business was named from a combination of electrical terms to form the name Camtron LTD.

Working with him was Bill Bain and the two of them loved motorcycles. Bain had an iron head Harley-Davidson Sportster, and Mike had purchased a 1964 Norton Atlas.

Having his own business, led to having his own shop in his garage, and back into motorcycling. He used his garage shop to make electrical panel, and the garage doubled as a bike shop.

Mike still had a great admiration for the bikers he had seen in San Francisco and wanted to customize his Norton. He began to remove and remake various parts. The handlebars were replaced with high-rise bars. The tank came off and was repainted. Gradually the Norton was beginning to resemble a custom or "chopped" machine. Some parts were simply taken off, and sent away to be chromed. The seat was a stock bench style with a hard English Naugahyde cover. Mike removed it and remade it to look sharp and be more comfortable. It was disassembled down to the seat pan or base plate. Mike wanted it to be more ergo-

Mike, his Norton, and his first custom seat

nomic and comfortable as well as look good. He cut the metal pan with a hacksaw and sandpaper to reshape it to his idea of how it should look. This involved a step being shaped into the pan. He then went to a carpet supply and bought foam padding. His next-door neighbor had an industrial sewing machine and stitched together a tuck and roll cover for him, which completed the make over.

The bike now looked different enough to attract attention. Everyone loved the makeover and especially the seat.

Bill suggested that they go to a rally. He said, "You have a customized bike now, so we need to go to a rally." Rallies in those days were reputed to be tough and if you rode a motorcycle going to them was a manly thing to do.

Rallies were all about drinking beer and getting in fights and kicking over some guy's bike. After all, that is what happened in *The Wild One.*

Mike and his friends were no different. Many times three or four of them would go to a rally and all stay in the same room, with the bikes. After all if the bikes were left outside they might be stolen. Hotel owners really hate it when bikers do that, but they'd often do it anyway.

Bill and Mike arranged to go to their first rally. It was a Norton rally in Grafton, New Hampshire, and they were going to be tough guys and go to that rally.

They rode to Grafton and the rally went well and Mike's modified Norton was a hit. Everyone liked the customizing on the bike. The real jewel on the crown was the seat and Mike was only too willing to tell how he came to create this new butt buffer. How he had taken the stock seat apart and reworked it for looks and comfort, then talked his neighbor into sewing the cover to his specifications, and re-attached it to the base. It was a good story, it looked good, and it rode great. Everyone at the rally wanted that seat.

One Norton rider kept badgering Mike to sell it. Mike argued back that he would have no way to ride home if he parted with the seat. Among the helpful suggestions offered by the would-be buyer was to fold up his coat and ride home sitting on the coat.

When the offer reached $40.00 Mike decided it was time to fold up his coat for the ride home.

Mike would encounter the man who bought the first seat several times over the early 70s and they would discuss his progress in the seat business. The guy once asked him where he came up with the idea to make and sell seats and Mike answered, "When you gave me the forty dollars for the first one."

Needing another seat, he purchased a new

one from the Norton dealer and set about making another custom creation for his bike. He took the new one apart and redesigned it, this time with a "Rat Tail" high back. Mike took the metal pan and had a friend weld the back to it giving a look that would later be known as a King & Queen style.

Once the stock parts were modified and the fabricated ones attached, he went back to the neighbor to get another cover stitched together.

Mike's friend with the Sportster now wanted one, but Mike protested. Making a custom item for yourself is a hobby, but making one for someone else is work and Mike was already swamped with real work. The electric business was going well and there was no time for seat making. Besides, he said, "I am not in the seat business. I am an electrical contractor."

Along the way, Mike had met Jean Louise Lara. She was working for Loring Labs as a color film processor at a photography lab where she operated a Kodak color-processing machine that required constant maintenance. Mike worked at Loring Labs part time as a technician servicing the electronics on these machines.

The two became acquainted and he discovered that she possessed a variety of talents including photography, office management, and bookkeeping. She left there to join Mike and helper

Jimmy McVitty and came on board at Camtron as the bookkeeper. Perhaps she was an ingredient needed to start Mike Corbin once more on the road to reinvention. Jean could do the bookkeeping and paperwork Mike needed which left him free to concentrate on actual work production.

Camtron LTD did well through 1966 and 1967. The Viet Nam War had become a giant eating machine and was devouring everything in sight. Labor was in an ever-shortening supply while the demand for goods and services was at an all time high. The war had not yet eaten the economic Popsicle down to the stick and funding was unchecked. Financially, it was a great time for the equipment suppliers and those who serviced the suppliers. It was a very lucrative time for the providers who stoked the war machinery.

1968 brought a new factor looming on the horizon.

Public opinion had gone decidedly against the war, and things would keep worsening as more and more American soldiers were coming home in bags, or maimed for life. Students on almost every college campus in the United States were protesting actively, and even Dr. Spock went public in an effort to influence the population toward forcing the government to end the war. Later this would erupt in violence at Kent State University in Ohio, leaving four students dead and nine others wounded.

In 1968, the presidential election campaigns were underway. President Lyndon Johnson announced that he would not seek election and the Democratic Party hastily turned to offering Hubert Humphrey as their candidate. Richard M. Nixon, a dark horse who was previously considered finished in his political career, skyrocketed back into the public eye as the republican candidate. This was an unprecedented chain of events and Nixon quickly became the one most likely to win. Nixon ran on the promises that if elected he would end the Viet Nam War. It seemed as if that campaign promise would work, and it did ultimately.

In addition to all of the politics, the work-a-day world still had to turn, and Bill still wanted a saddle for his Sportster.

One of the talents that would prove to be the hallmark of Mike Corbin's success was and is an uncanny ability to sense the winds of change and read into them which way they would blow. This ability has fairly faithfully served him well in anticipating which way the market would go in America and being able to have his efforts and products ready for the day of sale. In the case of 1968, Mike sensed that the glut of available work would diminish if the war ended. War's end would stop the need for war material as well.

Ultimately, it was this sense that was the catalyst in the mix that led to the future of Corbin, but some other things had to take place first.

Setting the stage for the transition from master electrician and hobbyist to businessman with goals was the pestering by Bill Bain for a seat and Mike's mom giving him advice.

Bain, also known as "The Blaster," wanted one of Mike's seat creations for his bike and finally obtained the leverage to get one. During a slow period when he was owed some pay for electrical work, he attempted to convince Mike to pay him in trade with a seat makeover. Mike gave in to this argument and made a custom solo seat for the Sportster.

Bill was soon showing the new seat configuration to Sal Scirpo who owned the Harley-Davidson dealership in Hartford. Sal was surprised at the style and quality of the seat and had never thought of Mike as a seat maker. He never knew Mike as anything but an electrician and motorcycle rider. Mike knew Sal as a really good all around motorcycle guy and the two liked each other.

Sal really liked Corbin's work and immediately saw the sales potential. Even though Bill assured him that Mike couldn't or wouldn't be interested in making seats, he contacted Mike to ask him to make some for the dealership. After negotiations that began with Mike's usual protests, an agreement was made that Mike would make five seats for the dealership at $25.00 each.

Mike got the seats made and delivered them to the dealership and collected a check. Mike laughingly remembers getting a parking ticket while he was inside delivering the seats and feeling lucky that he didn't have to spend his profits paying for being towed away.

This was on a Saturday and he killed some time running other errands before returning home. When he got in the house his wife said, "That Harley guy called you." Mike's first comment was, "Oh no, something musta' went wrong. Oh God, he wants his money back and I gotta go get the seats." He was mortified and thinking the worst about the situation.

His thoughts were that he finally had something to sell of his own; a real product, and he is about to be slapped in the face with the rejection of it. Reluctantly, he called the Harley shop, asked for Sal and timidly said, "Hey Sal, this is Mike, how are you doing." He did not want to hear the answer.

Sal said, "Oh great! What a day! I sold a bunch of bikes and I sold four of those seats and

I'm putting one on the shop bike. I'm going to go riding it tomorrow, actually, and I think that whole bike and that seat are sold too."

Mike said, "Wow! That's great I'm happy."

Sal told him to make ten more. Mike replied that he didn't think he could make more than five but Sal insisted on ten and said you'd better bring ten over here. With that and other orders, Mike became the Sportster seat guy of Hartford, Connecticut.

This unexpected success making these seats, coupled with Mike's fear that the war and subsequently his business would end with Nixon's election led to the seat business. It was developing on its own steam rather than by a conscious effort on Mike's part. Convinced that "Tricky Dickey" (the term of the times) becoming president was inevitable, Mike pursued making seats.

For a while, the Corbin seat business and Camtron LTD co-existed. He was delighted to be making things for motorcycles since they were his first love, and being in the motorcycle industry was even beyond dreaming.

But sometimes dreams do come true, and so it was for a young Mike Corbin, and the dye was cast. The demand for his seats increased, and he expanded his facilities at his house in Manchester, CT, to accommodate the demand.

Everyone wanted the war over in those days including Mike, regardless of his fears regarding loss of income. Mike was adding on to his ability to make custom seats. He was doing odd jobs, such as plowing the drive for the woman next door who, in return, taught him to sew.

He bought a Singer sewing machine and put it in the attic. He did a lot of work in his garage, but it was still primarily his electrical shop.

In the beginning, the seat bases were made of wood. This lasted about six months, but Mike realized that soon a method for creating metal-based seat pans would become necessary.

According to Jean, "Things were happening really fast and we covered a lot of ground in a very short time."

His mother provided the push that made the seat business official. She was visiting one weekend when Mike was really busy. He had expanded to envelope all of the available space in the house. He had his garage shop and the sewing machine was in the attic. There was a small electric heater up there, and the furnace in the basement kept that area warm so that he could use it to make parts. All of the area that Sue and the kids didn't have to use for living space had become workshop. Some of the seat production, specifically things like sewing some pieces, even spilled over to Jean's apartment to be completed.

By 1968, the point had arrived where Mike was known well enough that bikers would call and say I'm coming over on Sunday and get a new seat made for my bike and would just ignore the fact that this was Mike's home.

Mary saw what was going on with the house space and all of the guys hanging around with bikes waiting for seats. She told Mike, "You can't have all of these guys coming over to your house." She said, "You have three kids playing in the yard with these motorcycles going in and out of the drive. The cops are going to come here to see what's going on and the neighbors will be upset. You are going to have to have a business location." She insisted that he needed a place of business and a business phone away from his home and family.

Mary knew about these things, having worked for several businesses. She had even worked as a private secretary at Simplex Time Recorder for the son of the man who invented the time clock. She knew that he needed a real company and a company name. Mike agreed with her, and the realization set in that it had come time to make it a real business. He named the company Corbin Manufacturing, rented a real shop space, and the seat company was officially born.

Chapter 5
Corbin Gentry

Mike decided on the name Corbin Manufacturing for his new company and he was off running. His immediate space needs were met by renting a small shop on Charles Street, in East Hartford behind Right Way Electric Motor Company for $200.00 per month. This space was a 20 x 20 building and although it was only 400 Ft^2, it was a start. He had a product, customers, and now he had a location.

While Mike was arranging the new shop space, Jean had taken off on a road trip to call on dealers. She made a wide sweep southward, then west, and finally back north. She began the trek with her best friend Dorothy (Dot), but the two had to split up along the way. Dot was pregnant and was forced to return home early.

When Jean returned from her successful sales trip marathon, the shop was set up complete with tools and the commercial sewing machine.

More riders began to come to the new Corbin Company for custom seats. Dealers were beginning to order seats for customers and to have a few in stock as well. Primarily, they were the tall-backed banana seats on wooden bases and the Sportster solo seats.

He discovered that he loved working with his hands and creating his own designs. He derived so much pleasure from the enterprise that it hardly seemed like work.

Teaching himself to be a designer was similar to being a model maker when he was a youngster except that he was in control of defining what the product was going to be and how it would look.

It was thrilling to Corbin to see a bike going down the road equipped with one of his seats, and he couldn't get that imagery out of his mind. He

The Duster - the first Corbin seat

47

loved riding motorcycles, and now he had become part of the industry.

He had never before thought of that aspect of himself. His whole focus and plan up to this point had been to develop his career as an electrical contractor and electrical engineer. Suddenly, the realization hit that he not only can be in the motorcycle industry but also is actually there.

Almost unconsciously Mike decides to go forward in this industry and make it his life and career. To make sure that he has no choice but to make it work, he sells his electrical truck and tools so that he no longer has that option to fall back on. He decides that he wants to be fully committed to the motorcycle industry. This is a decision that, for some, might suggest that he ought to be committed in another sense of the word.

Without the electrical career option, he put himself in a make it or break it situation. With Camtron now gone, Mike pushed forward and says today, "I never looked back. I never wanted to be anywhere else after I figured out I could be in the industry that I loved."

He never forgot his love of electricity and his electrical background. This love is ingrained in him deeper than he realized at the outset of Corbin Manufacturing, and that will resurface later in a different guise.

The money from the sale of the tools and truck went to purchase equipment for making metal base plates. The previous seats had all been on wooden bases, and Mike wanted to add more products to his line. He bought a metal shear, drill presses, a welder, and some other tools and equipment. With the banana seats on wooden frames, he could make them by himself, but to expand, he would need more machinery than he had when he was working in his garage shop and more manpower.

After selling his newer truck, he ruined his old one hauling the heavy equipment that he had purchased for the new shop. Subsequently, he bought Jimmy McVitty's new green four-wheel drive Dodge Power Wagon.

Two of the three guys working for him at Camtron came to work for him at the new seat company right away. Collectively, they began traveling around New England visiting motorcycle dealers and getting them to look to Corbin for seat alternatives and replacements.

All was not smooth sailing for this ex Navy man and his new life. A storm was brewing on the home front. Mike's marriage to Sue was in trouble, and even though a fourth child had been born, there was no saving the relationship. Shortly after Mike's fourth and last child was born his marriage failed. By 1970, the couple was separated, and by 1972, divorced. Sue moved back to California, taking the children with her.

In addition to the two guys, Jean Lara had also made the transition to Corbin Manufacturing as the management and office functions person. With the other guys and Jean, Corbin had a workforce that was a winning combination. Together they would all make motorcycling history.

Not long after his divorce, Mike and Jean became involved romantically and were functioning as partners in life as well as in the business. Jean was already divorced and had a son of her own. Mike was the creative force as designer and inventor, and Jean was the one with the office skills.

They produced a brochure and began to mail advertising materials to motorcycle dealers all over the United States. Mike was so happy to have made it into the motorcycle industry that he dedicated his life to having no other career. He vowed to be the best at what he was doing in the industry. He says today that the smartest thing he ever did was see the tiger, grab it by the tail, hang on, and never let it go, no matter what.

Even though it was a new business, and was tentative, it was doing well. Winters were excruciatingly slow, business wise, but they always managed to make a few seats, at least enough seats to survive until warm weather and riding season came again.

A lot of veterans were returning home from Viet Nam and wanted to customize (chop) the metric bikes. Two major things happened to give a sudden and unexpected boost to the motorcycle industry. Honda developed the four cylinder 750 in 1968; the movie *Easy Rider* came out in 1969, culminating seven years of media and films bombarding a ready public, and as Mike says, "All Hell broke loose."

Collectively, there was suddenly the explosive rebirth of an industry. Everybody wanted a bike. This was the awakening of an entity, which until then, had been a sleeping giant.

After World War II, the industry had been fairly slow. The heavy bikes were holding steady, but not setting the world on fire. Indian Motorcycles was out of business by 1954. Harley-Davidson and Triumph owned the big bike market. Through the 60s, Harley-Davidson was averaging about 12,000 bikes a year and Triumph almost three times that number at thirty thousand. The Triumph Bonneville dominated the go fast market with its capture of the speed records that earned the bike its name. Still, the heavy bike market was almost miniscule when compared to other industries and the motorcycle market of today.

A seven-year prologue began, leading to a boom in motorcycling popularity, marked by film and media. This beginning is traceable to 1963s *The Great Escape.*

In 1963, the immensely popular actor and America's bad boy Steve McQueen starred with a host of others, in *The Great Escape*, a movie based on an event that happened during World War II at Nazi POW camp Stalag Luft III in March 1944. Airmen dug secret tunnels in a plan for 87 of them to escape. In actuality, only 76 prisoners made it out of the tunnels and fled the camp. Three made it to freedom and the rest were recaptured. Six of these were sent to other places, and seventeen were returned to Luft III. On Hitler's orders, the other fifty were taken to remote fields by the Gestapo and executed.

McQueen, an avid motorcyclist, insisted that a scene be written into the film where his character would attempt an escape by fleeing the German guards on a motorcycle. A successful escape would necessitate leaping two parallel barbed wire fences on the bike. In the actual event, no such motorcycle attempt was made and, in the film, McQueen doesn't make good his escape. The movie was very popular with the viewing public and added to the popularity and American pride associated with motorcycles.

By 1964, an opportunistic California political machine and a hungry press, eager for sensationalism, began bombarding the public with a constant stream of news about the Hells Angels. In 1966, the movie *Wild Angels*, a film loosely based on the Hells Angels, and starring Peter Fonda, Bruce Dern, Nancy Sinatra, and Diane Ladd was served to a public with already whetted appetites for motorcycle shenanigans.

In 1967, *Hells Angels On Wheels* was released starring Jack Nicholson, which also featured the rowdier side of motorcycling and outlaw clubs, as did *The Wild One* previously in 1953.

With the release of the movie *Easy Rider*, the American public at last had an "Iconic Image" of what choppers are, and what freedom really is. Again starring Peter Fonda, this time teamed with Dennis Hopper and once more Jack Nicholson, a waiting public witnessed a sociological statement about America and it changed our world. At least it changed the world for a lot of people and specifically the world of motorcyclists and the related industry.

The saturation of film and media culminated into a mix by 1969 that was on its way to becoming America's signature identity and all at a time when it was needed most. No one went to see *Easy Rider* only once, and in their heart of hearts all identified in part with Wyatt, Billy, and George.

With the disillusionment caused by the unrest over the war, America needed an identity fix, and *Easy Rider* was the provider. There were at least four other biker movies in 1969, but nothing on film of any genre captured the core of the American psyche the way *Easy Rider* did so easily.

While there had been only ten notable films of this genre between 1953 and 1969, the success of *Easy Rider* spawned no less than nine new films in two years, all attempting to capitalize on this sudden popularity of motorcycles.

The media and the movies contributed free marketing to the concept of bad boys on bad toys and made it an ideal. Honda came along and made it possible.

While the Honda didn't necessarily make the American market's most popular contest, it sure made sense. It didn't leak oil, had an electric starter, and good brakes. This bike was fast and reliable. It wasn't Captain America, but it was affordable and better yet, it was easy to customize. It changed the world of motorcycling forever.

Corbin immediately saw the potential and invented a seat and related hardware to fit this machine. He created a seat with a metal base plate and mounted it with a hinge so the seat opened to the side, providing battery access. Built into the seat was a fourteen-inch backrest. Mike patented the seat and it was a booming success. This side-hinged seat for the Honda 750 / 4 was the strongest selling single item that Corbin produced in the early 70s.

The Japanese had production down to an art and could produce numbers unheard of previously and marketed profusely. During the following years, they took the English bike companies effectively out of the American market.

The sleeping giant was awakened as life was breathed into the industry and Corbin Manufacturing blossomed. They couldn't make seats fast enough for the demand. As fast as they moved into one facility it was time to expand into another.

Corbin Manufacturing became a very prosperous company. Simple seats made way for other inventions, and those led to more inventions still. In the early seventies, Corbin had over sixteen patents on motorcycle seats.

A frame manufacturing division was started at Corbin in order to expand the company product line. The company was growing and adding to its product line without Mike having much control over the branding and brand image.

A whole gambit of Corbin titles, were applied by whoever was doing the talking in those days. Officially, the company was Corbin Manufacturing. To others it was Corbin Seats, Corbin Saddles, Mike Corbin, or simply Corbin.

The company had hired a couple of sales reps to travel and call on regional shops. One sales person, named Dave, would typically go the farthest afield. A Plymouth Duster company car was purchased for Dave to drive on these longer sales trips. Dave covered the New England and New York areas and did quite well getting seat orders.

The spring of 1970 found Dave heading farther south, expanding his range into Maryland, Washington, DC, and Virginia. The farther south he ventured, the less orders he was able to get.

Finally, he called Mike and said, "I am going into shops and when I introduce myself as Dave from Corbin, I am treated with a coolness I'm not used to encountering." He told Mike he thought the combination of being a Yankee, having a Boston accent, and out of state plates was frustrating any efforts he could make toward taking seat orders. He had decided that maybe they should abandon the idea of a Southern territory and just concentrate on the more Northern territory for the sales. Mike advised him to check in somewhere, get a night's sleep, and let him have a night to think about it.

Mike was on the way to work the following morning and listening to the radio in the truck as usual. One of the songs the radio station played was the 1967 hit song *Ode To Billy Joe* by Bobbie Gentry. This gave him the solution to the problem of the negative name association.

When Mike spoke with Dave later in the morning, he told him to change his introduction and pen in on his cards the word Gentry after Corbin. From then on, he was to introduce himself as Dave from Corbin Gentry and emphasize the word Gentry. Dave asked, "What's that all about."

Mike said we have to overcome the Yankee image, and Bobbie Gentry is a Southern girl and she is all South. She's a Rebel." He paused for a second and said, "And we are, too."

This ploy worked great. Dave reported that it was successful and the reception at each dealer went well, and seats were being ordered. Dave had cards printed while he was in the field and never stopped. He went all the way to Florida calling on dealers. Eventually Dave would be nicknamed, "Seat Sellin' Dave."

This was the company's first marketing position. Previous to this situation, they didn't know that they had to make statements about their brand and identity. It was now clear that they had to make it known that they were Corbin Gentry from Connecticut and they made seats. No one argued, the seats sold like crazy, and this was their first experience at branding. When they actually incorporated in April 30, 1970, it was as Corbin-Gentry, Inc.

They learned everything the hard way, but Mike recalls that they were great times for him and the company.

By 1971, the Corbin Gentry catalog was beginning to show numerous products for motorcycles beyond seats. Handlebars, sissy bars, frames, and frame accessories were offered and all for a variety of bikes. All of the more popular models of Harley-Davidson, Japanese, and British bikes were represented. There were over 35 types of seats alone in their product line. The seats began to have tough names, which inspired images of speed, power, and a lethal tone.

Mike was inspired to create macho type names because Craig Vetter had named his products similarly. Craig was famous for his innovations and inventions in the 60s, and Mike held him in great esteem. Vetter had named his innovative windshield the Windjammer. Riders didn't have to say windshield at all. If in conversation parts were mentioned, a rider only had to say

"Windjammer" and everyone knew what it meant. Windjammer just had a great ring to it.

Mike's seats had previously had names like Minstrel, Gold Digger, and Skipper. The new models had monikers such as Invader, Blaster, named for Bill Bain, and most fierce of all, the Widowmaker. What's in a name? In marketing Mike discovered, everything.

Later Mike would use this discovery coupled with America's love affair with the Old West and a seat called Gunfighter would become the biggest seller and most imitated motorcycle seat in the history of the industry.

Over time, they outgrew the Manchester shop and moved to Bolton, CT and into a 1200 Ft² facility. From Bolton the company moved to the Ellington, CT, airport and into their first wholly occupied building, which was soon outgrown and then it required an addition.

During the short time they were in Bolton, Al Simmons, a former dirt track racer, joined the company in sales. Al had been partners with his brother in the racing effort, but had a child and needed steady income. He wanted to stay in motorcycling, so he responded to an ad for a sales person at Corbin Gentry offering the opportunity to earn thirty to fifty thousand dollars per year.

Someone else beat Al to the job, but lasted

only a week. Once Simmons was acclimated to the product line, he discovered a talent for sales he was not aware that he possessed. Al was the player

Al Simmons working in sales

that was needed to complete the team. With Mike as head of design and production, Jean as office management, and Al in sales, Corbin Gentry was unstoppable. Al would stay with the company for another nine and a half years before leaving to start his own seat company, Mustang, which is still doing well today.

Mike gives Al credit for being passionate about motorcycling, his salesmanship, and for being "a quality guy." He says that he and Al have shared a lifetime of mutual respect.

No one could have foreseen the explosive growth of the industry in the early 70s, or the similar growth of Corbin Gentry. Along with the industry, Corbin Gentry kept pace with a constant increase in staff, product line, and sales. They now had distributors at various locations around the country and a Pacific division located in San Francisco.

The company was headquartered in Ellington for about three years and had added a dealership for Triumph, BSA, and Rickman motorcycles. By having a showroom, Mike was able to spend a great deal of time talking to riders and gaining a better understanding of what was involved in being a dealer. This experience made it easier to talk to other dealers with a clear sensitivity to their needs and that boosted sales greatly. Knowing the life that a dealer had to live helped to raise the bar on how the products had to fit, look good, and arrive in a timely manner.

Corbin had designed one of the first aftermarket rigid frames for building choppers without having to use modified stock frames. It had a low center of gravity, whereby the engine could be kept at or below the normal crankshaft height. These frames had a stretched neck and lengthened down tubes in order to have the chopper-look while maintaining a low center of gravity. This is the way most choppers are made presently, but Corbin was the first to develop this concept. The rigid motorcycle frames for a variety of bikes and custom trikes was a new concept at the time. Before these frames were developed, the practice was to bolt or weld on a rigid rear section or "hard tail" as they were called, and a long extended front end to achieve the desired look. With this method, the center of gravity was thrown off and up and the engine tilted back. The result of this altered geometry was to adversely affect the balance and, in the case of the Triumphs, create oiling problems for the engine. They made the hard tail add-on frame pieces, also, and made them to fit all of the more popular bikes for customizing such as Sporsters and the big Harley 74s.

Everyone wanted a bike that looked like the ones in *Easy Rider*. These were rigid Pan head Harleys built by Dan Haggerty (Grizzly Adams) specifically for the movie. There were not enough used Harleys around to satisfy the exploding market and demand. Builders were forced to look elsewhere. The most popular ones, by far, were the Triumphs, and Corbin Gentry sold a huge number of those.

The bestseller in rigid frames, were the ones to fit the Honda 750s. Everyone wanted the rigid chopper look, but liked the idea of using high tech engines. The Hondas, were reliable, affordable, and, best of all, they were available.

This was a very fun era Mike recalls and during this period Mike honed his skills in designing in and working with metals and welding. He also learned his most valuable lessons in managing people and marketing.

The company was doing well enough that

Mike considered taking advantage of an opportunity to buy the Ellington Airport, but a better situation presented itself, which was to alter the direction of the business and Mike's life. He would return to his roots and begin again to work with electricity.

Along the way, Mike and Jean became a permanent committed relationship, and he became virtually a stepfather to Jean's son, Morris. Mike had a deep love of kids, and being absent from his own most of the time, he quickly became close to Morris and was raising him, with Jean, as his own.

There was another youngster involved with Jean and Mike. A boy from Costa Rica named Alvaro Figuroa. Alvaro was a foreign exchange student who resided with Mike and Jean.

Alvaro and Mike became quite close and Mike felt as if he was almost another son. Alvaro learned a great deal with the Corbins and enjoyed his stay with them, but inadvertently had to return to Costa Rica sooner than expected due to the death of his father. The boy's family was in farming, and his father was killed in a freak accident on a tractor. Alvaro had to return to help support his family. He was able eventually to finish his education and earn a degree in agriculture. He developed an interest in seed production and exporting and today has many holdings. He has become one of the world's largest import-exporters of fruits and vegetables and owns the highly successful company, Fruita de Internationalé. Mike speaks even today of the pride he feels over having been a positive influence in Alvaro's life. Alvaro and Mike are still close and keep in contact.

Morris still works at Corbin Gentry in production and management with Jean. He is one of the owners and customizes seats for a better fit to bikes and riders. Bike owners all over the US send seats to Corbin-Gentry to have him rebuild them. Morris grew up in the motorcycle industry. He and Mike have not maintained the close relationship they once had.

Work was great and the company was growing faster than even they could fathom. It would seem that the seat and accessory company located at the Ellington Airport would grow until it consumed the airport itself.

In 1974 things would begin to change for Mike, Jean, and the growing company as well as the rest of the country. This was a change that would bring electricity back into Mike's life. The nation had entered into a recession in November 1973. There was an Arab oil embargo and truckers went on strike.

A surprise opportunity presented itself to the company and they seized it. Corbin-Gentry acted

on a chance to acquire a huge facility. They aban-
doned any thought of expanding further at the airport and purchased an old woolen mill in nearby
Somersville. This mill had 225,000 Ft^2, a stream
running right through the center of it, and best of
all it had an old water turbine.

Corbin-Gentry facility in Somorsville

Chapter 6
Making Sparks Fly

The Somersville Woolen mill was like a castle with its immense size. The chance to buy the old mill was presented to Mike by a friend who dealt in real estate. Mike recalls that his friend was know as "Three Fingered Louie Lavit." Louie convinced Mike that he could get the mill and he turned out to be correct.

Purchased in 1974, the mill had enough space to do anything they could want with, or in it. Business was great and growing. Mike reflected, "We were in Camelot and didn't even know it."

The excess room in the mill made it possible to take production to new levels and it also made it possible to experiment, and when the 1974 Corbin-Gentry catalog was printed it foretold of new directions for Corbin.

The 1974 catalog states a cessation of distributors, which was necessitated by the growing need to provide dealers with faster access to good service and parts. Offered instead of distributors are three warehouses listed. One is at home base in Connecticut, and the other two located in Dallas Texas, and, of course, the Pacific Division in San Francisco. Additionally, is the disclaimer that Corbin-Gentry will not sell retail but only to dealers. This effectively was a non-competition clause.

Corbin Pacific of today maintains a similar attitude. While they will sell to retail customers, they do not allow discount sales outlets to compete with the retail sales of their dealers and themselves.

In addition, the 1974 catalog featured 34 seats, one less than the 1971 book. There are four bolt-on hard tails, seven full rigid chassis, and three trike frames. There are sections with a variety of handlebars, sissy bars, and miscellaneous parts. Not seen in previous catalogs were custom oil and fuel tanks, and a noticeable addition was the first emergence of fiberglass fenders.

The last page of the catalog has nothing for sale but the most unusual item of all, an electric motorcycle.

This was to be a harbinger of the future of Mike Corbin and a radical change in his philosophical outlook.

The last page must have caused more than

one dealer to scratch his head and mutter, "What in the hell is Corbin up to now?" The last page is only pictures and captions. At the top is a caricature of Mike, Jean, and an unknown crewmember. Mike is astride an electric powered bike and in huge letters underneath is Bonneville. No other explanation is there, or necessary.

All the world knows the name Bonnevile as the salt flats about a hundred miles west of Salt Lake City where the land world speed records are attempted annually.

The photographs show Mike sitting on an electric bike and is captioned that it is he waiting in line. Next down shows Mike and Jean standing  between two bikes. Caption says it's the two of them after grabbing two world records. The last picture is the whole crew, including all of the kids, and the caption is "World records take a good team."

Mike and Jean after winning 2 world records

Nothing for sale there, but there is a foretelling of the future both immediate and distant.

A world situation had taken place that would directly affect the United States where it

Mike at Bonneville

World records take a good team

hurts us most. We were hit directly in the pocket-book and more specifically where we live most dearly. We were hit in our transportation system and at the gas pump.

A series of events took place, which very seriously affected America by disrupting daily life across the board. While unforeseen over here, the die was cast when the Yom Kippur War broke out between Israel and the combined forces of Egypt and Syria on October 6, 1973. The United States and other Western countries supported Israel, which provoked OPEC to implement an oil embargo on October 17, 1973.

President Richard M. Nixon launched Project Independence on November 7. Encouraged by the

71

success of the Manhattan Project (The Atom Bomb), Nixon was determined that American industry, with the help of science and technology could free us from dependence on imported oil. Nixon stated that the energy crisis caused by the embargo, which once seemed distant, was rapidly closing in on us. He announced to Congress that America was facing the most acute energy shortage since WW II.

Although many gas stations had already been closing on Sundays to ease the strain on short fuel supplies, by December 31, 1973, Nixon announces standby gas rationing and by Jan 2, 1974, institutes a nationwide speed limit of 55 miles per hour.

Oil consumption had become 69% of America's energy consumption by 1972 and from 1970 to 1973 increased at a rate of more than a million barrels per day each year. While the production of oil domestically and through traditional suppliers had stabilized, the increases had become dependent on Arab oil. From August 1972, and August 1973, United States dependence upon Arab oil had increased from .38 million barrels per day to 1.1 million.

By February 1, 1974 there is a nationwide truckers strike and violence erupts at the nations terminals and on the highways resulting in two deaths. Gasoline theft was rampant across the nation.

By the middle of March, the strike is over and the embargo is lifted, but the damage has already been done. OPEC had not only disrupted American life, but it also paralyzed most of Western Europe's production, and earned an additional $100 billion dollars in the process. Even though the embargo had been lifted and the strike stopped, the recession, which had been triggered by the OPEC actions in November of 1973, lasted until March 1975. The US GDP dropped by 4.9% making it the worst economic setback in the US since the twin depressions of the 1930s.

Mike Corbin was already working on solutions without knowing it early in 1973. His electrical background was in play and working in his inventive mind.

The new mill home to Corbin-Gentry straddled a stream and had a millpond to go with it. The original woolen mill was powered by a water turbine, which turned the looms and other equipment. Mike and crew had removed the old turbine from the waterway and restored it to working condition. They purchased a surplus Navy generator that had been in service on a destroyer and attached a belt drive system to turn it with the turbine. Now, there was a way to electrically heat part of the mill with a completely renewable energy source.

This tied in nicely with Mike's love of electricity and his interest in the possibility of electrically powered vehicles. His previous experiments with electrical power and the success at Bonneville were about to take Mike and the company on a new tangent.

While Corbin-Gentry was located at Bolton Mike had begun experimenting with electric power for motorcycles. Using a Ford starter motor as the engine, he built an electric mini bike. This experiment worked out well enough that he made six of them and managed to sell five to motorcycle dealers.

Armed with the success of the mini bike experiment, Mike decided to build full sized electric bikes and prove their viability. With the success of the Ford starters in mini bikes, he knew that he could make his machines work but would need much bigger electric motors. Inadvertently, the military once again was the answer to

Electric mini bike

fulfill the need.

Just as military war materials for jet engines provided the work for Mike's career as an electrician, a similar source was the solution to full sized bikes. The answer to a need for large motors was found in some experimental military jet engine starter motors with very sophisticated motor windings. The first of the large bikes are the two that were taken to Bonneville in the summer of 1973. These set new records for two wheeled vehicles running on electricity. Mike rode one bike and the other machine, was ridden by Jack Wilcox. Named Jumpin' Jack Flash and the Magnificent Electric Machine, these were fitted with the experimental motors and lead acid batteries. A record of 101.867 miles per hour was set on the salt using all electric power. They had done it.

Mike believed that they could do better and planned to return the following August with more power and go for a higher speed record.

The OPEC oil embargo late in 1973 was just the circumstance needed to provide necessity and inspiration for the birth of invention. Corbin did not miss this opportunity, and he went to work developing an experimental bike viable as a production motorcycle. Mike was a great admirer of Soichiro Honda and dreamed of developing a production machine and achieving a success similar to Honda's. Soichiro Honda once visited the Cincinatti trade show in the 70s. H looked into the Corbin Gentry display and had an assistant tell him in English that he did nice work. This was a very inspiring moment for Mike, who said to himself, "What Honda is to motorcycles, I can be to electric vehicles." "Perhaps," he thought, "the electricity-powered motorcycle would be the fulfillment of that dream."

The first prototypes were developed early in 1974, and after rigorous testing, and the inevitable bugs worked out, provided the knowledge of what components would work together and function on the road.

A second prototype was built and licensed for road use in order to prove reliability. It seemed that an electric powered motorcycle that would pave the way to a solution to the fuel crisis was practical. The proof would be at hand soon. Life changed forever when, once again, the reinvention of Mike Corbin would take place because of the appearance of a new player in his life. Charles MacArthur walked in and invited him to lunch.

MacArthur, familiarly known as Charlie, was an environmental scientist dedicated to the research into the development of lower energy technology. He had been seeking ways to get around the dependency on Arab oil. Charlie had long held that a single passenger vehicle with an electric drive would be the best answer to the long gas lines and elevated prices. A rumor reached him that a guy was building an electric scooter, or something like that, in Somersville, Connecticut. The rumor was that the guy up there was named Mike Corbin and was working out of a recycled mill complete with a dam and turbine you could walk on. This sounded like a project worth supporting. He decided to go and see for himself.

Mike had not quite finished the motorcycle, but Charlie thought the electric bike was really neat and worked out a trade. Charlie had recently developed a way to make hot air balloons operate more efficiently by aluminizing the interior of the bag to create a thermos bottle effect. This reduced the fuel use by a factor of four. They agreed to swap a balloon for an electric motorcycle.

Charlie who had not ridden a motorcycle for over twenty-five years was now the proud owner of the first Corbin electric bike aptly named the "City Bike." Taking it home would catapult Charlie and Mike to a higher level in their efforts and relationship.

The City Bike was small as motorcycles go. The production model was equipped with a two horsepower Baldor motor. It had a nineteen-inch front wheel and an eighteen-inch rear. The front rake angle was steep at 27.5°. Much of the bike was standard fare with Honda hubs and Red Wing front forks. The frame was conventional tubular steel, which by now Corbin-Gentry was well adept at producing. The steep rake and 52.5 wheelbase made the little bike turn on a dime. At least its less than eight foot diameter circle was a dime in the realm of motorcycle specifications. All things factored in, the costs per mile were about two cents.

While Mike continued with development and business as usual, like Mohammed, Charlie was going to the mountain. Mount Washington that is.

Charlie decided to visit some friends in New

The City Bike

Hampshire and decided to take the bike with him on a trailer. Passing Mount Washington, near the town of Gorham, he read that this hill was 6,288 feet high and had grades as steep as 22° in places along the road to the top. "This," he said, "is not a mountain. This is a granite dynamometer." It was

Electric Street Bike Crew delivering the first production bike to Charlie MacArthur (center without sunglasses), with Mike (front),and Al (second from right)

quickly decided that this mountain was a perfect place to test the mettle of the electric bike.

The management told Charlie that it was OK to give it a try and that the auto road was a private drive. The drive took three hours to go the eight miles. Half way up to the top, however, the batteries were dead. Charlie discovered that a twenty-minute wait would rejuvenate the batteries enough to proceed once more. After three hours, Charlie walked into the lower lot at the top with the bike beside him going at full throttle. It was pulling its own weight but not with Charlie mounted on it.

He was elated. He had made the summit and "damn it" had proved it could be done on an electric vehicle. Being a scientist, Charlie quickly calculated that the three batteries on board had done about two and one half million foot-pounds of work to get the bike to the top. In spite of having to walk it the last leg of the way, the "Little Bike That Could" did it under its own power.

First electric climb to Mt. Washington

Charlie was really excited over the possibilities and felt his beliefs had at last been vindicated. Once he'd returned to the bottom he talked to the site manager about the accomplishment. He had formulated an idea while on his way back down. He felt this would be a fantastic place to have a contest. His idea was to invite other inventors and environmentalists to an event, which would test their creative abilities to develop vehicles designed to do the most work with the least expenditure of energy. The contestants would have to make it to the top and back down on a measurable amount of energy. The one using the least would win an award.

The manager agreed and said OK, and it could be held the following year. It was planned for June 19, 20, and 21, 1974, the first days of summer.

Nineteen contestants entered the event and all three major networks were there to film the contest. With the country still in a fearsome state of mind over the recent energy crisis, it was a very newsworthy event.

One added perk for Mike was the developing lifelong friendship with Charlie MacArthur. At the marriage of Mike and Jean on December 30, 1976, MacArthur was the best man. Today Mike credits Charlie with changing his life and philosophy. Charlie, who has dedicated his life's work to making the world a better and more environmentally conscious place to live, has had a profound influence on Mike. Mike developed a similar dedication to the environment because of the influence of Charlie, but not quite to the extent that drives the passions of MacArthur himself. Mike says today, "Charlie MacArthur was the most influential person in my life. He changed my life's whole philosophy and direction."

Not long after the first Mount Washington event, Mike and crew were back at Bonneville's salt to try for another speed record powered by electricity.

This trip to the salt was with the assistance of Yardney, Inc. of Pawtucket, CT supplying the batteries. Yardney was a company that produced high-powered batteries for the Military and the US space program.

In 1973, traditional lead-acid batteries powered the record setting Bonneville runs. These batteries were good, but not able to deliver enough power to the electric motor. Mike was able to attract the interest of Dr. A.W. Petrocelli, Ph.D. Dr. Petrocelli was the General Manager of Yardney, became interested in the project, and like Mike, was interested in dispelling the myth that electric vehicles were slow, unable to climb hills, and could not go very far on a single charge. He authorized the company to produce some special high-powered batteries just for the Corbin-Gentry project. The Yardney batteries were a silver-zinc creation from torpedo batteries, and able to deliver a much stronger bolt of electricity. People standing near the bike without insulated shoes reported that they were receiving a shock through the conductive salt. Electrolysis was so great that you could almost see the corrosion form on the copper fittings. Because the batteries were made with silver plates inside, the bike was named Quicksilver.

Mike's friend Tony Sardinas, now a Wall Street Software Representative, was at the Flats as part of the crew. Tony was a bike builder himself at the time and had worked with Mike in the design and development of Corbin-Gentry's Café Racer frame for Harley-Davidson engines and their trike frame. He was a science and experimental type of guy like Mike and Charlie MacArthur and helped Mike with the rebuilding of the water tur-

Mike with Dr. A. W. Petrocelli

bine. Tony vividly recalls the days at the Bonneville Salt flats and the things they had to do to make the runs the second day and later get back home to Connecticut. The battery straps, according to Tony, were copper bars about ¼ inch thick, because conventional wire couldn't hold up to the extremely strong electric current. Recharging the batteries for the next day's run was a problem also. These batteries consumed a lot of juice to recharge, and there wasn't enough time to recharge overnight on the 110-volt power available to Mike and his crew.

One of the guys, called Black Jack, climbed the power pole and tapped into the power company's transformer to get enough voltage to charge the Quicksilver's batteries. The transformer was the one feeding the motel with electricity, and tapping into the power source caused a slight brownout to the motel. This was August and they were at the edge of the Mojave Desert and it was hot out there. The batteries to the bike were topped off, but the motel air conditioner's compressors began to burn out and fail due to the voltage drop to the motors.

The trip home wasn't without incident either. The gasoline rationing was still in effect and Mike's huge motor home was a gas-guzzler. With rationing, filling stations were supposed to limit fuel to ten gallons per vehicle. This behemoth could hardly get around the block on ten gallons of gas, much less from Salt Lake to Connecticut. They made the trip home by Mike having to bribe station attendants to sell them enough gas to fill up.

Tom Corbin, who was still a child at the time, remembers the trips to Bonneville with his dad, as a great adventure. He and the other kids were on a trip of a lifetime for kids their age.

The new bike, which had two jet engine starters, was able to set a record of 165.387 mph, making Mike Corbin the fastest man in the world powered by electricity. The first run out was at 161 mph and a final run of 191 mph was achieved, but not repeatable to establish a record. Since that record was set in August of 1974, a faster record with electricity has been set with a four-wheeled vehicle. The record for two-wheeled and electric-powered set by the Quicksilver bike with Mike Corbin on board still stands today.

By now, Mike was getting used to being involved with setting records. At the 1975 Mount Washington event, a Corbin production bike sporting one of the Yardney batteries was able to set the record there. Mike set the record by reaching the top in a blistering, relatively speaking, twenty-six minutes. In second-place, an electrically powered V W. made the climb in a little over an hour.

No other vehicle was able to complete the climb to the top.

Mount Washington has another unique characteristic. The mountain has extremely high prevailing winds at the summit. In 1934, the observatory at the top recorded the highest velocity wind ever observed by man at 231 mph. Corbin and Yardney engineer, Steve Schiffer, used these winds to their advantage by placing an Enertech wind generator near the top to produce enough to recharge the battery for the descent.

It was at this point that Mike began his foray into the world of four-wheeled transportation on electricity. An automotive platform was needed that could be powered by electricity and Mike took on that project for the Mount Washington Hill Climb. The event now had an official name, which was The Alternative Vehicle Regatta. The actual prize awarded was called The Tom Swift Award. The award was named for the scientist, and inventor hero of the children's serial adventures by the same name.

For the following year, Mike devised a jet engine starter motor set up, similar to ones in the land speed bikes, to replace the engine in a Volkswagen with the body panels removed. The contraption was just the pan, two seats, and the running gear. He fueled it with eight lead-acid golf

Mike's bike at the top of Mt. Washington

cart batteries and rigged up an on/off switch for a control and the driver eased the strain by slipping the clutch.

Charlie and Mike calculated that although they could use the motor as a generator coming back down the mountain, it would only be able to restore about a third of the energy. To solve this problem, they again placed the wind generator at the top and used it to recharge the batteries once the vehicle reached the summit. Charlie's daughter, Deborah, drove the vehicle and the result was another record because the stripped down VW had the same amount of energy on board when it reached the base of the mountain as it had when it started the ascent.

More experimenting followed, and the Corbin-Gentry Company inadvertently had discovered a new niche - electric car conversions.

Mike's son, Tom, remembers those days very well. He takes a great deal of pride in telling of watching his dad both at Mount Washington and at Bonneville, checking out the routing.

Mike, it seems, would get up at daybreak and walk or run the route to find, and feel with his own feet, the best ground to ride for the best traction and least effort for the vehicle. Tom says he vividly remembers Mike jogging in a zigzag pattern the full length of the run at the salt flats to discover if there were any soft areas, which should be avoided during the run for the record.

There was now a new product in the Corbin-Gentry line. This time it had nothing to do with motorcycles except that the test bed for the concept was from developing the City Bike and its success on the road and the mountain. The best new thing was engine conversions for VW Beatles to make them electrically powered. The company developed kits and instructions to make it possible for customers to purchase everything needed for a person with mediocre skills to convert a VW Beatle over to electric power. There were a couple of different configurations, but the basic version called for replacing the rear seats with batteries. Other arrangements were possible if a client wanted to retain the back seats. Accessories included a battery charger, a last chance switch, for both cars and the bikes, and of course, the inevitable seats. The conversions featured two configurations. One was a basic version with eight batteries and the other available in a twelve battery set up.

The bikes also came in two versions. One was a single speed for $1,395.00 and the other a two-speed for $1,495.00. The basic car kit was $1,549.00

Company growth was charging ahead with the addition of the electric vehicle department, and the team of innovation, management, and sales seemed to have the ability to attain any heights they desired.

Jean drove one of the car conversions in the Alternative Regatta. The brakes overheated and the ride down the hill took over two hours with stops to allow them to cool. It was a scary experience at the time, she recalls, but speaks of it humorously today.

For one season, Beverly Hannan, Corbin-Gentry's production manager, drove a company owned VW conversion. Her son had wrecked her

Electric Bug

Plug Into Standard Outlet

GO ONE STEP FURTHER — BE TOTALLY
INDEPENDENT ! RECYCLE A "BUG"

A VW converted to electric power will pay for itself.
Cost of operation is half the price of gasoline. Kit is
applicable to all models of rear engine VW vehicles. Recharge from a standard household 110V outlet. Cruise
40 to 45 mph for 35 miles with 12 batteries. The VW 4
speed transmission and clutch provide a simple but very
smooth control of speed and acceleration without the
energy losses associated with resistor type or electronic
controllers. The flexibility of the kit allows the builder
to choose the right battery combination for his own
needs. The basic 24 volt, 8 battery package will give a
range of 30 miles at 30 mph with a top speed of 45 mph.
Higher voltages will increase top speed. Batteries are
most easily installed in place of the back seat. This keeps
the car balanced for safe handling. Plans include full size
templates for cutting the plywood. The builder may de-
cide to use his own imagination and retain the rear seat.
There is room for 6 batteries behind the seat.

The remaining batteries could be carried in the front
trunk and in the motor compartment. Weekly maintenance required is simply to check batteries for water level.
Windshield wipers, radio and lights run from an auxiliary
battery. Simple, neat, clean installation with plans fur-
nished. Can be dealer or factory installed. Register as
an electric vehicle in any state. It meets all standard
safety regulations. Everything you need to convert your
VW to a useful, economical reliable electric car is included. 78% of Americans travel 18 miles per day. If you
are in a traffic pattern within the capacity of an electric
vehicle, you owe it to yourself and your environment to
travel conserving energy. No fumes, tune ups, spark
plugs, or noise. Low initial investment, maintenance and
energy consumption. Corbin-Gentry believes electric
vehicles are part of the future. We're making our investment now. Price $1,549 for Basic Kit as shown.
Options include gauges, safety disconnect switch, and
additional batteries.

Battery Exhaust Fan   #A1FAN   Battery   #A106
Battery Bus Bar Set   #A1BUS   Emergency Disconnect #A1EPD

Contactor Assembly   #A1CONT
Drive Motor With Flywheel Adapter #A1DM

Motorplate With Throttle Bracket #A1MP
Cooling Blower   #A1BL

Battery Charger   #A1CHR
Optional Instrument Package #A1INST

Replacement
Front Seat Custom
Upholstery Fits VW
Beetles 1956-1964

VW Front Seat Covers
PN VW 1

LAST CHANCE SWITCH

A new emergency power disconnect switch named the "LAST
CHANCE" has been developed for electric vehicle applications.
The spring loaded knife is your assurance of control in any emergency
situation. The "LAST CHANCE" is opened by a mechanical remote-
mounted cable mechanism. Levers are available for electric vehicles
with handlebars and tee handles for dashboard mount applications.
This E.P.D. has no electrical dependency to function. Compact styling
professional finish, quantity discounts and OEM prices available.

Corbin-Gentry, Inc.

40 MAPLE STREET • SOMERSVILLE, CONNECTICUT 06072 • (203) 749-2238
11305 INDIAN TRAIL • DALLAS, TEXAS 75229 • (214) 243-7264

Electric Volkswagon Bug Article - 1974

car and it was taking an inordinate amount of time to repair it. Her car situation, when coupled with the fuel crisis, created ideal circumstances for the company to test the conversion beetle in a daily distance commute. The company needed research data such as mileage, kilowatt-hours, and how the car performed under actual conditions in the wintertime. Hannan kept written records of the data for the company's research. She fondly remembers the added bonus of getting into a car on frozen mornings that was already warm and had no ice to scrape from the windshield. The batteries being recharged overnight kept the inside of the car nice and warm.

The new electric car conversions drew the attention of the Governor of Connecticut, Ella T. Grasso. Governor Grasso was very supportive of enterprise in her state, and with the fuel crisis, she wanted to showcase this concept. Corbin-Gentry built her a conversion to drive and display, but instead of a VW Beatle, they converted a Chevrolet Chevette.

The seat and frame divisions continued to do well and continued doing business as usual. Seats increased in product line and sales and the company grew accordingly.

By 1975, the company had expanded in size and in products. Mike had an insatiable appetite for inventing new things and specifically in keeping the seats abreast with the production of new motorcycle models.

1975 was to be a pivotal year for the company growth and its beginning diversification of products, particularly those electric in nature.

The catalog cover was still devoted to motorcycling but now the cover was the color picture of Mike setting the record on the Bonneville salt. The picture wraps around the entire book. The front cover has the Quicksilver bike in the wind, and the back has insert pictures of the bike and a production bike at rest.

The number of seats had increased to 40, and there were two more frames. Among the 10

Electric bike production line

sissy bars is one with a chrome auxiliary fuel tank and the addition of the XLP-11 electric production bike for the first time. This bike will later be named the City Bike. The catalog advertises that this bike will operate on .06 cents per each 30 miles. The last page of the book has the Quicksilver again along with a picture of nine XLP-11s being assembled in their new electric production division.

By 1976, the catalog again had a full color cover but this time the Yardney sponsored Mount Washington bike was on the front, and Mike, fly-

Mike setting the record on the Bonneville salt

ing in his hot air balloon, was on the back. On the inside is a pen and ink sketch of Mike and Jean sitting on a hillside. The product line is similar to previous catalogs with the addition of the electric vehicles, fiberglass fairings, and now the number of seats is sixty-six plus the two VW seat covers offered.

1976 closed with the wedding of Mike and Jean after almost a decade of building a business together like no other ever seen in motorcycling accessories.

Corbin-Gentry began 1977 with an even bigger line of products in its catalog and an expansion of the electric vehicle division. The car conversion kits were being produced with a higher voltage package, which meant a longer range and a higher attainable speed. The generator providing electric heat for part of the mill was now doing double duty to charge batteries for the vehicles as well.

Bike frames increased from seven to ten over earlier product lines. The fairings were dropped, but Captain's chairs and mounting hardware for vans had been added. Motorcycle seats in the catalog were now up to ninety-one and it appeared that things could only get better and the company richer.

Mike and Jean built a large house on a hill over looking a great view and at night could see the lighted sky of New York. The house bordered the edge of the Snipsik Forest and this provided both privacy and an advantage for the couple, Mike in particular. Mike had always been a mid-pack marathon runner, which had stood him in good stead for covering the miles of salt at Bonneville and the road to the top at Mount Washington. Living in this location gave him access to the fire trails to run with the family dog, an Airedale named Guinness. They ran in the early morning hours to keep up his stamina and distance ability.

The electric car conversion kits were selling well, and they were generating a great deal of revenue for the company. The electric bikes, however, were not doing as well as expected, although over a hundred were sold.

For 1978, the seat line had increased to 115 in the catalog along with a new car conversion kit. The Chevette conversion that had been produced

Electric Chevrolet Chevette

for the Governor was now a kit offered to the general public. Mike was working with the Baldour electric motor company to produce a proprietary motor for the Corbin-Gentry conversion kits and electric bikes. This motor was to be a 72-volt, 20 horsepower power plant, but it was never to be.

There was a hint in the wind of some things that would not bode well for the Corbin-Gentry electrical vehicle division. With the end of the embargo on Arab oil, fuel prices were falling and gasoline was available in plentiful quantities, and the gas pumps were back in business at full tilt. The romance and desire for alternative energy systems and electric transportation were beginning to wane, and the American public put the fuel crisis behind them and relegated it to the status of a bad memory.

A new craze was beginning to take hold in America. The word "Macho" became an everyday term and movies were being cranked out of Hollywood by the dozens. Charles Bronson, star of *The Magnificent Seven, The Great Escape,* and in 1977, *Raid On Entebbe,* was enjoying a run of playing macho movie characters. Three were in 1977 alone. Sylvester Stallone stared in Rocky and FIST. Karate Champion Chuck Norris was already starring in his fourth feature film.

In 1977 international weight lifting champions Arnold Schwarzenegger and Lou Ferrigno became household names by starring in the movie *Pumping Iron.* Ferrigno was catapulted into American living rooms by being cast as the green monster in the enormously popular TV show, *The Incredible Hulk*. This show was based on the already well-known Marvel Comic Book character, and ran from 1977 to 1982.

Almost overnight, bodybuilding became an American pastime if not an obsession. This was a trend once again not missed by Mike Corbin, and Corbin-Gentry entered the workout machine industry. During 1978, Mike who was already an amateur weight lifter, teamed with Donald Schoeck to develop the prototypes of an arm curl and rowing machines.

Mike became almost as interested in constructing and marketing the bodybuilding equipment, as he was the motorcycle equipment. As the last year of the 70s began, Mike, perhaps unknowingly, was taking something out of the decade with him. The influence of Charlie MacArthur had impregnated Mike's own mental makeup and infused the two friend's philosophies. The man, however, Mike wanted most to emulate was a closer likeness than Mike realized. For like Honda, Mike embraced the concept that an innovator must have an appreciation for nonconformity. In an added comparison, Charlie MacArthur and Mike Corbin, like Soichiro Honda passionately believed that technology must live in harmony with ecology.

Chapter 7
Changes In Attitudes Changes In Longitudes

No one could have predicted the turn of events that would affect the company and Mike's life over the 1979 calendar year. The United States was in a recession left over from the Nixon years and Jimmy Carter was now president, but the fuel crisis was over and gas was plentiful. While this was good for the economy, it was not good for the electric car and motorcycle business.

The American public had become far less concerned about gas prices than whether or not there was gas available. This attitude was reflected in sales at Corbin-Gentry in that the electric part of the business began to slow down going into 1978. People wanted vehicles that had speed and range capabilities greater than electric technology could provide. With crude oil no longer in short supply, and no more rationing of gasoline, the public went back to driving as usual.

The economy being as it was, had caused a side effect that also affected the electric motorcycle and car kit business. Inflation was up to much higher levels than anytime since 1970, reaching levels of 8.45% in 1973, and then 11.37% by 1974. Unemployment remained stable during the fuel crisis, albeit with a slight dip in 1973, then began to rise in 1974, and almost doubling at 8.48% in 1975. Inflation began to climb steadily back in 1977, reaching 12.3% in 1979. The unemployed, and those in fear of becoming that way, do not buy new vehicles as a general rule. The return to pre-1971 levels would not happen until 1997.

Climbing unemployment, coupled with high interest rates and plentiful petroleum fuels, sounded a death knell for the electrical division of Corbin-Gentry. During their time in production, the electric motorcycles and car kits sold in the hundreds. Mid to late 1978, the remaining stock and parts were sold to Ray Lyman of Lyman Electric which brought to a close the Electric Production Department formed only three years earlier. Mike Corbin would never lose his attachment to electricity or his devotion to development of alternative transportation and renewable energy.

Going into 1979, the company was centered around the continuing creation and marketing of motorcycle seats and accessories and began to turn a large portion of its attention to the relatively new diversification of its line of body building machinery.

This was a line of equipment that Mike had a great deal of interest in developing. Working with Don Schoeck over time, they produced and marketed a wide variety of machines.

The team of Corbin and Schoeck began designing the prototypes and testing them in 1978, but the first starting order for steel and parts to build a production run of twenty arm curl machines wouldn't go out until January 29, 1979. The machines worked quite well and attracted the attention of the fitness giants who were making news with the rising popularity of bodybuilding. The machines were used by major figures such as Russ Warner and Arnold Schwarzenegger. Arnold was enjoying a huge following because of publicity and movie appearances. Martial arts films and the ones featuring men and women who were making careers of pumping iron had struck a chord with the American buying public. Corbin-Gentry was there with the machinery and the production facility to keep up with the demand. The company would become a primary sponsor of the I.F.B.B. Mr. Universe and Mr. International Contests, which were produced by Schwarzenegger and Jim

Lorimer in 1980.

All in all, the teamwork of Mike's design capabilities and Don Schoeck's engineering would produce no less than eleven radically different machines and related equipment. The two men would

Mike with Arnold Schwarzenegger

each hold patents with the designs, in addition to many patents Mike held within the motorcycle industry and for electrical devices. They developed machines that functioned in a system that they termed "Bio-Mechanical Synchronization". They began with an arm curl machine then designed a rowing machine, and followed with weight equipment such as stands and press benches.

The Corbin-Gentry expertise was able to provide never before comfort in the seating areas of the machines. The first machines were followed

101

by a second rowing machine (B model), a chest press, leg, calf, hack, and deltoid machines. The leg machines were a leg curl and extension machines.

Mike and Don seemed to be the perfect combination of genius to make these machines possible. The interest came from the fact that Mike was a marathon runner in the mid seventies and developed the problems in his back and legs indigenous to that type of athletics. The two men were able to determine that existing machines were incompatible with other parts of the human body even while they were helping strengthen the areas for which they were intended. While building muscle in the legs, for instance, there might be knee joint damage occurring simultaneously. They were not synchronous with the whole body area being developed. This seemed contrary to the way the machinery should work, and so, Mike and Don decided to pool their expertise and create machines that would do the job correctly. Achieving the ideal would mean that an area could be worked hard, but with little or no joint or skeletal damage in the process.

Don was able, through his engineering expertise, to design a way to evaluate, or measure as it were, the strength of a particular body part geometrically through the whole range of motion when lifting or moving weight. They discovered when this system was applied, that each body part exhibited an entirely different curve of characteristics from any other. Mike believed, then as now, that to properly design anything that has to function beneficially for human beings, it must be done from the bottom up in order to work properly. This method had always worked in the proper design of seats, and these machines were no different. They also determined that a major flaw in existing machines was the lack of fluid motion, which created sticking points and linear loads.

The concept they designed was named Bio-Mechanical Synchronization and meant that there was a way to achieve physiological harmony between the machine and the body through the entire range of motion. Thus, a specific muscle group could be developed to its maximum capacity with little or no injury if worked properly.

On a side note, in addition to body building equipment, the company created a bicycle seat for women named the Voyager. This seat was configured with two pads to cushion each bottom cheek and was available in two colors and in a choice of Naugahyde or leather. The optional leather seat was an additional $10.00.

The machines, like the seats and the electrical devices, worked almost perfectly, and the little company that started with one sewing machine and $80.00 was worth millions and doing well. Mike wasn't happy, however, and had begun to grow more discontented. The team of Mike and Jean was beginning to crack at the seams.

Each had done his or her part and had done them to an almost super human level of excellence. Mike, with the inventions of new products, and Jean, providing the administrative expertise, and the two of them, coupled with Al Simmons' salesmanship, had built a business that now had over a hundred employees and experienced a meteoric rise to success. The rise to success was a learning experience for both of them. Mike states emphatically that Jean learned to be an excellent business director, and could run a business almost without peer, at least in that type of business. He also says that he learned how to be an inventor.

He says, "It was really two different challenges. I didn't have much appetite for business. I didn't have any ability, education, or desire to go sit in an office and learn how to run a business." Mike prefers, still, to be the hands on design and production person.

From the outside, it must have appeared to be a nice world of success, enviable by all observers. The world was fragile like fine porcelain and had tiny flaws and cracks beneath the surface.

For Mike it was coming apart. There was the inevitable conflict that seems to always exist between creative and administrative forces in a company. One is always seeking the sublime in creativeness, while the other is seeking the best bottom line on the financial ledger, and each one thinking that it is their part that carries the greater level of importance. Differences of opinion between Mike and Jean as to the directions for the company, and necessary production facilities for the future were an issue as well as the nature of product development.

Besides the inevitable conflict in the work place, there was trouble in Paradise on the home front. While enough money was not an issue, and the couple lived in an ideal home by the forest, their marriage was coming apart anyway. Perhaps, even, the cracks were stress cracks from the strain of such an endeavor, and the immense time and labor required to get that far in such a short period of time.

Other factors were at play influencing the winds of change beginning to blow into Mike's life. A variety of things all converged at once to direct life-altering decisions including disappointment with the demise of the electric part of the company. There was the growing feelings of estrangement from his children. He was close to Jean's son Morris, but that wasn't quite the same as being able to spend more time with his own.

There were also other circumstances, which made California appealing to Mike. Mike's strongest suit has always been being possessed of the ability to make a keen observation of market conditions. By observing the conditions and following the patterns of direction, much the same way that weather is tracked, he had discovered that it is possible to predict where things are going in the market. This is true at least a significant portion of the time. By learning to pay attention to these patterns, it is possible to be ready for the market and have your products available when the day of sale is at hand, rather than being behind the curve and thus, too late to be effective.

Mike had been making regular trips to California, both to see his children and keep check on the Corbin-Gentry Pacific Division, which by now was in San Jose. He spent a great deal of time with friends out there and borrowed bikes to ride around the area. By being directly exposed to the San Francisco area riders and lifestyle, he was able to see the changes gradually taking place in the industry.

One friend Mike visited regularly was Tracy Nelson, who owned a company named The Fiberglass Works, located in Santa Cruz. Mike would always somehow end up at Tracy's place. Tracy was well known for his unique designs and was a part of the motorcycle culture in the Bay Area.

Mike learned, by hanging around with Tracy, that the area was the most eclectic Mecca in the country for motorcycle acceptance. All of the major brands of bikes were accepted there, and by virtually all riders. During this time, while seeing and experiencing the motorcycle world in the Bay Area, he began to realize that by being in Connecticut, he fell short of the degree of immersion in the motorcycle industry as he would like to be.

The San Francisco area and surrounding vicinity was a stronghold of Hells Angels, which provided a lot of inspiration, as well as the large number of café racers riding California Highway 1. Many of the café racers were Triumphs and Hondas that had been "fixed up" for that kind of riding. In addition, the bodybuilding industry had pretty much settled on the west coast. There was a lot of exciting activity going on in many arenas and all of this convinced Mike that he needed to move to California. He knew that his feelings were not shared back in Connecticut and his marriage, in his eyes, wasn't anything he could cling to any longer. He didn't think that the way things were going was the way he or Jean should spend their lives with each other. He says readily, "it wasn't anybody's fault, it just fizzled out."

In spite of the level of success, he made the decision to leave Connecticut. The recession made it a little easier to justify, but it was still hard to do anyway. Mike felt that things needed to change. The Corbin-Gentry products were still great quality items, but the rigid choppers were going away, or at least partially so. The era of the Honda and Triumph rigid frame and bolt on conversions was ending in favor of different directions in motorcycling.

Mike was trying to find out what was going to be the next rage in motorcycling and be able to be there ahead of the curve. Being in a little town in the country all the way east in Connecticut made it hard to keep your finger on the pulse of the industry and motorcycle design. Mike was sure, in his own mind that California was the pinnacle of the way design was going. There was as much going on in Southern California, but his ties were in the northern half of the state. In addition, his kids living there was a tremendous incentive.

The recession had caused interest rates to jump sky-high and times were really tight, but a new kind of motorcycle was emerging which had the promise of great things for the future of the industry. These were Japanese machines that looked like racing bikes.

Mike was sharpening his mental tools, watching the changes around him, and planning, once again, to reinvent himself to fit in to the budding new era of motorcycling. Mike made up his mind that it was time to leave, and so, he separated from Jean and the eastern half of the company as well, for all practical purposes. Mike wanted to buy Jean's half of the business, but she was not interested in selling. In order to reach some kind of reasonably equitable agreement, Mike agreed to sell his half to Jean for whatever terms were doable for her. He agreed to settle, in part, for the Pacific warehouse in San Jose and left to head west. A division of personal property would come later and would include an African Gray Parrot named "Dirty Mike."

Splitting from Corbin-Gentry left him with very little money. He lived in a motel room for six to eight weeks and then settled into a small, single bedroom condominium in a Santa Cruz High Rise, and began what seemingly was a backwards career move to being a company distributor selling Corbin-Gentry motorcycle seats, accessories, and the line of exercise equipment.

Splitting the company he had literally started from a toolbox was terribly stressful and saddening, but Mike was determined to make it work. It wasn't a completely peaceful split. "It never is," says Mike, "It's like cutting a pyramid of oranges in half in the grocery store. It doesn't work, and all you get is oranges all over the floor."

Needing all the available cash that could be mustered, Mike sold his three Triumphs and two Harley-Davidsons. With that done, he prepared to leave Connecticut for what would be the last time with the exception of return visits on business and to visit family.

With a tremendous sense of failure and loss, he made the move, bringing with him his Yamaha XS-850 Midnight Special, a Honda car, his personal Snap-on tool box, and started all over again with a new life.

Chapter 8
Reinventing Corbin

The balance of the fall of 1979 went by quickly, and Mike wasted no time in taking over the Pacific division and the rented warehouse that served as both storage and sales office. He began calling on dealers and selling seats. There had always been a manager in place out there, but he had not been aggressively pushing the business, or at least not to the degree that Mike felt was needed. The company had never done the amount of sales and marketing that was possible by being an absentee company running a California division from Connecticut. Mike was about to change that since part of the buy out of his half of the parent company was to take products in lieu of cash. These would need to be sold rapidly in order for him to survive. He terminated the manager after about two weeks and took over managing it himself. Mike stated he never realized the importance of Al until he moved to San Jose and had to get out and sell products himself for the first time in his life.

Mike entered 1980 with a burning desire to make his move to California the best decision of his life. His intent was to pursue selling the body-building equipment as much or more than anything else, including seats. He wanted to do both, however, and made a lengthy attempt to do so. His contacts in the industry proved to be sound and much publicity was generated with the help of some of the heroes in the iron pumping business.

1980 would see the success of the machines go so far as to appear in many of the magazine write-ups. Corbin-Gentry would have the endorsements of such stars of the West Coast bodybuilding world as Arnold Schwarzenegger and Dennis Tinerino appearing in Corbin-Gentry ads and posters. Dennis would be in many of the magazine ads promoting the equipment. Tinerino held the titles of Mr. World, Mr. Natural America, and twice was Mr. Universe.

Mike became fast friends with Russ Warner, the former Mr. Hawaii turned fitness guru and equipment dealer. Russ became the main west coast distributor for the machinery that Corbin-Gentry produced. In addition, he was a consult-

Advertisement featuring Dennis Tinerino

Advertisement featuring Arnold Schwarzenegger

ant for Mike in the business of selling bodybuilding machinery, Mike's running partner away from the business, and the two spent a great deal of time together.

Seats were not left behind with the concentration on bodybuilding machines. Motorcycles were still Mike's first love and during the early eighties Mike made at least three trips back to Connecticut to design more seats for the company's production line, both for him on the West Coast, and other dealers and distributors.

One of those distributors was Mustang Seats. Early in 1980, after 9 ½ years with Corbin-Gentry, Al Simmons left the company to become a distributor as well. Al says that he just needed to go into business for himself if only to preserve his sanity. It was the right time to take himself to a higher level in his career and make the move. He actually planned to be one of Corbin-Gentry's distributors, somewhat similar to what Mike was attempting.

Al says he left in good graces, but later when supplies of products were stopped, actually said to Jean that he would become her biggest competitor. Initially, things went well, but keeping Al and Mike both supplied with inventory was straining the limits of the Corbin-Gentry production capacity, and Mike had priority. This effectively cut off, or at least back, on the availability of inventory. Out of necessity, Al bought the equipment and facilities of SMC seat company in Palmer, Massachusetts and then began producing his own line of seats. He named his new company Mustang Motorcycle Seats and began production in June 1981. He worked hard and managed to make it on his own. He was able to survive and debuted his new seats at the 1982 Dealer's Expo Show in Cincinnati, Ohio. Al's company gradually took over the number one spot in market share as Corbin-Gentry gradually declined in sales. Mustang Motorcycle Seats became, and are still, one of the largest producers of motorcycle seats in the world.

Al's departure, which closely followed Mike's leaving, would remove two of the three original team players, which collectively had produced the energy that was responsible for the meteoric rise to the success level the company had reached. Neither Al nor Mike would remain distributors for very long.

From his new office, Mike made rounds and made phone calls to dealers, ad-nauseum. Initially, Mike's son Tom worked after school, on weekends, and through the summers. Tom was Mike's first employee in the new company, but before very long a couple of additional sales guys were hired, as well as a temporary girl as office manager. He had plans to just to be the West Coast sales rep and his business plan went no farther than to be the Western Division Distributor. Buying the condo left him pretty much broke, and he knew he had to sink or swim with his sales of seats and equipment.

After about a year of operating as a Corbin-Gentry distributor, Mike encountered a previous problem. The situation, which had originally plagued the company's West Coast distribution, was still a problem, even with him on the West Coast handling things. The logistics of having products produced in the East and delivered to him in California in a timely manner still existed. It seemed, for some reason, that coordination between the California warehouse and the Connecticut plant facility was never able to synchronize efficiently. His ex wife was controlling the production and routing of the products, with a major portion slated to go to her ex husband. They were never able to get that relationship to develop into a profitable cash flow for either of them.

It was becoming clear to Mike that he would have to get involved once again with the design and production of the products. Mike could see that the turning pattern of motorcycling, which was becoming a faster and faster paced cycle in the industry, would necessitate a more rapid ramp up coupled with a much shorter time to market than was possible with the existing system. To do this, he needed to form a new corporation that was separate from Corbin-Gentry. He no longer owned the rights to the name Corbin-Gentry, but also needed the name recognition of Corbin. He called his new company Corbin Pacific, and the plan was to expand but still be a Corbin-Gentry distributor. So, after twelve years the Corbin name as a brand was reborn with the reinvention of a concept for successfully creating a product to supply a waiting target market.

Part of the continued association with Corbin-Gentry was very successful and due mostly to the development of a new bike by Yamaha. This new motorcycle was the Virago, and it was a hot item. As soon as these bikes hit the street, Mike had a seat design for them, which was one of the projects he went back to Connecticut to develop, and these seats sold wonderfully, as did the bikes themselves on the West Coast. This was one of the first times that Mike designed a seat for a bike right off the assembly line which has been a mainstay ever since for Corbin Pacific. This bike had a huge following that still exists to the present and almost revolutionized the cruiser market in America.

Mike was beginning to realize that he had

surmised correctly, and the need to develop products would have to be done faster and more efficiently or it would not be possible to bring an item to market in time for the needed day-of-sale. The seats traditionally manufactured at Corbin-Gentry were produced on a 16 gage steel base plate with reinforcement bars, which in of itself created several problems impacting production ramp up time to day-of-sale. Number one, they are fairly heavy and number two, the industrial investment required for new models is quite high. Cutting and forming machinery is necessary along with die sets for each seat model base plate.

The Japanese motorcycles were dominating the market, and were, as Mike puts it, "coming out with new models every year, crazy fast." The pace had begun in the late seventies and kept increasing annually. Every year would see five to eight new bikes on the market.

Inflation was rampant and interest rates were up to 18-20%. Mike was under capitalized already, and it seemed as if it would be impossible to get enough money to tool up and make new steel base plates fast enough for the California market, notwithstanding that even if the funding was there, they could not be produced quickly enough. He felt that the modern seats would have to be built on fiberglass bases and that Corbin-

Gentry would not be willing to convert over. Even with the large facility and staff, Corbin-Gentry couldn't keep up with this new pace. His opinion was that Corbin-Gentry, without Al and himself there, was being directed from the top down, rather than the bottom up, and being managed by business people who did not ride motorcycles. There was no conduit from the company to the riders.

Mike was passionate about motorcycles, as was Al Simmons, and as long as they were there; a finger was being kept on the pulse of the industry, which was no longer present. Mike readily credits Al's salesmanship with being a major force in making Corbin-Gentry a huge player in the motorcycle industry. As part of his passion for motorcycles, and an interest in improving the quality of the seats and accessories, Mike went to rallies and kept up a dialog with the riders and could interpret their needs and desires for products.

To Mike it was apparent that Corbin-Gentry was not keeping up with the changing times. In his opinion, with business people running the company who didn't see the necessity of spending money on motorcycles, or spending the time riding, connecting, and talking with riders, it had isolated itself enough so as to not see the metric sport bike coming into the future as a dominant force. Back at the plant in Connecticut, they weren't riding motorcycles or participating at events and standing toe-to-toe with the other motorcyclists. The glitch, or flaw as Mike saw it, was tied in with the question of how well do you interpret the market from a walnut desk? The answer is, "Well, you can't."

The dilemma appeared as a wall that could not be breached by the small new company, Corbin Pacific. He was painfully aware that he would have to do it all himself in order to be successful. To compound matters, sometimes products were shipped to him that he considered dead inventory, as settlement of the debt rather than fresh products suitable for the growing California market. He felt that the distribution company could have been a good business but not if Corbin Pacific couldn't get up to date products and particularly when needed.

With all of these factors in mind, and the necessity of getting products designed and to market in a timely manner, and ready by day-of-sale, Mike decided to take a different approach to resolve the situation. He tried to make the warehouse into a production facility, but couldn't get favorable zoning. In order to take advantage of the wave of lighter, faster, and sportier bikes coming on the market, Mike opened his own industrial-zoned production facility in the nearby town of

Watsonville.

He had a good knowledge of fiberglass production from the fiberglass division at the Corbin-Gentry plant and the fenders and trike bodies produced there. He bought used fiberglass and foam equipment from another seat manufacturer he knew in San Fernando. The company was called Hang-2 Seat Company and they had some older equipment no longer being used in production. His original intent was to buy the company, but that deal never materialized. Mike bought this equipment, moved it to San Jose, and later to Watsonville. He refurbished it as he had done with the old water turbine, a few years earlier. Other machinery was fabricated or bought in a worn state to save equipment costs and refurbished.

Once he had the plant in Watsonville operating and the fiberglass equipment working he began to design and make seat base plate plans and invented the liquid poured seat molding technique for which he still holds the patent. Late in 1981, he produced his first new seat since leaving Corbin-Gentry. Corbin Pacific, Inc. was finally open and operating in production of its own products.

Using his new company as a base, Mike was selling existing Corbin-Gentry designs and the bodybuilding equipment. He actually planned to use his facility in Watsonville to create the fiberglass-based products and treat the distribution of Corbin-Gentry seats and weight machines as a secondary business.

Leading into the 80s, things appeared to be well in hand. Back East, Al's company, Mustang, was a distributor, as well as Mike's new company, and between them things seemed to be covered both east and west. Much advertising material was being produced both by Mustang and Corbin Pacific and all factors, for all practical purposes, were doing well and operating in a compatible relationship. The most notable exception was that Mustang did not handle any of the fitness equipment.

The year 1980 had been a struggle for Mike financially and emotionally. With a vengeance, however, he dug-in and decided he was going to make a success of his endeavor regardless of the circumstances tossed his way.

He was selling seats as well as the bodybuilding machines, and trying to do both was taxing for the new again entrepreneur, but he never allowed the depression to get the better of him. His son, Tom, remembers seeing how depressed and disappointed Mike was that his marriage had not worked out and how hard this transition was to endure. Most notably, Tom observed that he never stopped working as hard as ever and always maintained his sense of humor regardless of the depth of the adversity. Survival was the paramount issue for 1980.

1981 would prove to be pivotal year for both Mike in California and Al at Mustang. Even though they were both technically still distributors for Corbin-Gentry, by the 1982 Dealers Expo Show in Cincinnati, they each had produced products not originated by Corbin-Gentry. The more the original company struggled to keep Mike in products, the fewer they were able to get to Al for Mustang. In June of 1981, Jean informed Al that the company was eliminating its distributor program and they would not be able to ship Mustang any more seats. Necessity became the mother of invention once again and this time the invention ultimately was two different lines of motorcycle seats. In order to have products to sell in the interim, Al contacted the other distributors, informed them of the change in policy at Corbin-Gentry, and bought out their inventory of Corbin-Gentry seats.

Mike continued to ride and attend the big rallies and dig into the needs of riders and how he could address those needs and do so profitably. Mike reflects on looking at the Harley-Davidsons on Main Street at Daytona and wondering if they would make the transition into the 80s. This period of time was during the time of the buyout and just before Harley-Davidson's Cinderella-story rise to market dominance.

By the close of 1981, Mike had pretty well decided on the direction he was going to take with his new business and he was beginning to believe that he could do better selling just seats, and especially his own seats, rather than trying to split his time and efforts three ways. Other things were about to happen in Mike's life as the new Corbin Pacific Company went into 1982.

Seeing that the market was changing, Corbin visualized how his new line of seats needed to look, and he believed he had identified the need for these products. Instinct and experience made him feel strongly that there would be a good financial market for the new seats he was preparing to produce. The dilemma between his new company and Corbin-Gentry was now working to his advantage, or at least forcing him to change directions and once again reinvent himself and his business.

His theory was that to be successful, his primary job must be to discover what product the company needed to make, by intelligently examining the motorcycling rider market, anticipate where it was headed, and have the right products ready when the demand is there. His strategy was to begin with one new item at a time, perfect it, and develop the marketing.

Mike's personal and business life was about

to change drastically. 1982 would bring more sur-
prises than he had bargained for, but they were
good for him and his new enterprise. The first of
February, Mike was back at the Dealers Expo in
Cincinnati and spending time there with the other
people from Corbin-Gentry. One of those people
was Beverly Hannan, the company production
manager.

Beverly, or Bev to those who know her, had
been with Corbin-Gentry for quite a few years. Bev
was from Holton, Maine, and had moved with her
husband and six children to Connecticut and had
been there twenty-two years. She had started at
Corbin-Gentry in 1971. Prior to 1971, she had
worked a few jobs but mostly stayed occupied raising her children. She needed steady work and began at the seat company in the shipping department. She would work for a half day in shipping
and then the latter half in the office. The seventy
five year old bookkeeper began training Bev in
accounting basics, which led to course work in
night school to become a bookkeeper.

After the company moved from Ellington to
Somersville, Bev worked as the shipping manager
for quite a number of years, then moved up to become the plant manager. She says that she worked
almost every job in the company over her eleven-
year tenure at Corbin-Gentry.

She, like Mike, had separated from her marriage by 1981 and was going through a divorce. The two knew each other quite well, having worked together for so many years. With both of them now single, for all practical purposes, Mike asked her out while they were in Ohio for the Dealers Show. They discovered that they liked each other and Mike suggested she go for a change of scenery and move to California to work with him at Corbin Pacific. Bev liked the idea and later decided to take Mike up on the offer. After her last two kids graduated from high school, she moved to San Jose to begin work as the office manager of Corbin Pacific. The two began in earnest to get the fledgling company off the ground and flying. Having a person in the administration that was dedicated and devoted to the success of the company, freed Mike to concentrate on product design and creating new projects. Bev took care of the books and helped in sales as well as all other aspects of the business administration. The two lived in Mike's Condo in Santa Cruz and commuted to the shop in San Jose.

It was a severe change for the two of them, both of which left a company with about 125 associates, and failed marriages, to attempt a new start-up. Today Mike says that he believes that failure is one of the stepping-stones of successful entrepreneurs. Rarely one will strike it lucky and succeed on the first try, but there is always that nagging fear that it is totally luck and it will be catastrophic if the luck goes away. After surviving the first failure, however, you have another attempt and the second time is easier because you develop confidence and have learned not to make the same mistakes made in the building of the business the first time.

In the forefront of Mike's mind at the time was the belief that the present products would not work in the 80s. He had been aware of this feeling early on and was perplexed about it. A number of things bothered him, not the least of which, was that Corbin-Gentry didn't have a design department with him gone, and therefore, the product line hadn't reinvented itself. At the turn of the 80s, as the motorcycle world began its change, their product line was being left behind. The result, at least from a West Coast perspective was that the product line was aging out.

It was the couple's leisure time and a fated Sunday afternoon, which was to change things for the little company and change them drastically. Mike and Bev traditionally took a customary country ride up the coast on Sundays to Alice's Restaurant on Highway 35. Alice's was, and still is, a motorcycling tradition in the San Francisco Bay area. It is a spot where motorcyclists of all ilks come to gather, eat, drink, and talk motorcycles. Alice's restaurant was constructed in the early 1900s originally to be a general store supporting the logging industry in the area. It earned something of a reputation as the local area which eventually became known as "Four Corners". It ceased to be a store in the 1950s and was turned into a restaurant. About a decade later, the restaurant was bought by one Alice Taylor, who promptly renamed the restaurant after both herself and the hit song of the same name by Arlo Guthrie. During her ownership, the restaurant acquired world fame as a stop for motorcyclists riding the curvy and winding wooded roads of the area. It also became a favorite stop for hikers and tourists visiting the area. The restaurant and outbuildings were acquired in the 1970s and since then have been family-owned and operated. It is still one of the bay area's most popular weekend destinations.

It was one of those rides in late 1982, while Mike and Bev were sitting on the deck of Alice's Restaurant, that he came up with an idea which was to make motorcycling history and create a product so popular that virtually every production seat maker in the US would eventually copy and is still the most popular style seat in the industry. This history making seat design was called The Gunfighter. It had the look and it tapped into the psychological attachment that every American motorcyclist has with the image of the nineteenth century American West.

Alice's Restaurant

Mike had adopted the tough sounding names after being inspired by Craig Vetter's Windjammer fairing, and the concept had served him well back when he was making Blaster, Invader, and Widowmaker seats. It would serve him even better now.

The end of the bolt together chopper industry of the 70s was ending and no where was this more readily apparent than in Northern California where all makes of bikes were accepted. Corbin-Gentry had tapped the chopper industry in the

70s and their business was built around that phase of motorcycling. Most had been British and Japanese, with some Harley-Davidsons in the mix also.

Now, the horizon was dotted with bikes of a new breed and lots of them. The Touring bike was born in the 70s with Honda's Gold Wing and others. Reliability and comfort were the most desirable features and Corbin-Gentry had made touring seats for them. The Japanese were once again taking the lead in the 80s, with Honda's Saber V-4, the 750-F, and others. Mike was beginning to make seats for these bikes with his new fiberglass base and poured foam technique.

Mike and Bev were at Alice's Restaurant on a Sunday afternoon just sitting around with friends talking about motorcycles and seats and looking at all the bikes in the parking area. There was a Honda Saber in view and Mike kept looking at the bike and trying to figure what it needed to set it off from other bikes. He visualized a different seat design, which would go with the racy style of the bike and paint scheme. Gradually, the Gunfighter seat took form in his mind. He worked out the specifics and created the first one for the Saber, and by early 1983, had the key to let out the biggest success item he had ever created.

These seats were just what these race looking bikes needed and they were immediately popular. Not too long after the Saber, Honda brought out the Interceptor. This bike was a radical departure from your typical street bike. It screamed out that it was a racing bike, but was nevertheless a street bike. Most were two tone and either in blue and white or red and white, and all, with a very uncomfortable vinyl seat.

This bike simply begged for better ergonomics and more color. In short, it begged for a Gunfighter seat.

The seats were two-toned with a white tail to go with the white of the paint scheme. It looked like a solo seat, but actually had enough padding behind the driver for a passenger. These seats sold like wildfire and Corbin Pacific began to enjoy a rise of success, which was totally unexpected.

By mid 1982, it became very clear to Mike that having the time to do all three of his intended business directions would be impossible. He would have to focus only on Corbin Pacific, Inc. seats exclusively. As much as there was good income in the bodybuilding equipment, the seats had the potential of generating the most income and in the shortest period of time. Orders to Corbin-Gentry and the sales of their seats, accessories, and workout equipment dwindled to nothing at all by 1983. Corbin-Gentry reports that even though the bodybuilding equipment was going great guns in 1980,

"The physical fitness without the California sales effort sort of faded away." Corbin Pacific, Inc. gradually severed all ties with Corbin-Gentry during 1983. On November 21st Mike and Jean's divorce was final, bringing a 16-year part of Mike's life to a close.

Mike and Bev continued to go to rallies and had discovered the rallies to be a never-ending source of both sales and exposure. The couple co-drove to events and set up with a truck and display.

Bike Week at Daytona Beach, Florida, was the most lucrative rally attended and is still that way today. Mike says that being at Bike Week every year has been responsible for half of his all-time rally sales.

It was at Daytona Bike Week in 1983 that was to become one of the most fortuitous incidents of Mike's career. He left the motel and was walking up Main Street. It was a pleasant evening and Main Street was lined with bikes, which is normal for all large bike rallies. This year many more Harley-Davidsons were in evidence.

In 1981, the Harley-Davidson senior executives had purchased the slowly moving company, which like its other American manufactured peers, seemed to be near extinction. Many thought that Harley-Davidson would follow Schwinn's Excelsior,

Henderson, and the ill-fated Indian into oblivion; relegated to being artifacts of American history.

This was not to be the case for Harley-Davidson, which like the proverbial Phoenix, leapt from the expected ashes of its demise to become one of America's greatest success stories. To begin with, the company began making machines that were more reliable. The Super Glide, designed by Willie G. Davidson, was released in 1971, which created a bridge between the Sportster and the large touring model FLH Electra-Glide. The Super Glide had more of the light Sportster type frame, but with the large 74-inch engine of the bigger bikes. In 1979, the motor company presented a receptive public with the FXS 80 Low Rider. This creation, fitted with a new 80-inch engine, was really sporty in appearance and came designated with the new name Low Rider. Corbin-Gentry had been making seats for these bikes and by 1983, Corbin Pacific was; also.

In 1983, Harley-Davidson pulled off a major coup when President Ronald Reagan, in order to help the Wisconsin company get an edge on the Japanese motorcycle companies, imposed additional tariffs on imported motorcycles with 700cc or larger. This gave Harley-Davidson an almost exclusive reign over the big engine market. 1983 was also the year that Harley-Davidson launched the greatest marketing strategy in motorcycling history. It founded the Harley Owners Group. This was a factory sponsored membership club with benefits and club affiliation through dealerships all over America. This was revolutionary in American business and although motorcycle clubs were anything but new, the HOG Club was without precedent, and still is. The concept was an old one, developed in Germany to skirt around government restrictions on providing discounts and benefits to selective people rather than have to across the board.

Worldwide membership has grown to over half a million and climbing, creating unbelievable loyalty to the brand and a captive buying public large enough to support the company.

Mike Corbin's foray down Main Street led to his observance that all of those Harleys were outfitted with seats of 70s style and vintage. Many were Corbin-Gentry, some were Corbin Pacific, and others were stock or from some other seat company.

Mike looked at these bikes and wondered what could be done to bring these seats out of the 70s, create change, and at the same time create a new product line for Corbin Pacific. The answer was simple and it came on him so quickly he was amazed, just from standing there on Main Street at Daytona looking at the Harleys at the curb. The answer was the Gunfighter, but designed specifically to blend with the look of the Harleys. It would be nice and wide in the front. The seat would hug the rider with low back support and a sweeping off tail that went back to the mounting bolt and seemed to disappear into the fender. He could visualize the new look of the seat while standing there. It would be a seat that could fit right on the stock brackets of a Harley and change the look of the very bike itself.

He went home and got on the seat development right away. He borrowed a Sportster and an FX from a couple of friends. Once on the market the seats were the rage. Everybody wanted one. Mike went to Custom Chrome and showed the seats to owners Nace and Ty, who liked them and decided to carry the seats. Overnight, Custom Chrome became Corbin's largest customer, accounting for 35% of sales volume throught the 80s and into the mid-90s. The company had to work day and night to keep up with the demand. Corbin seats were on the map in a spurt of exponential growth Mike could have never anticipated. No one else at that time had them except Corbin, but that would change within about three years.

It seemed impossible to saturate the market as it was and then Harley-Davidson came out with two new models, which served only to add fuel to the flames. The FXR and the Softail were both debuted in 1984.

The FXR was a beautiful handling machine and it had a whole new engine design, which was also rubber mounted for a smooth ride. The Softail was really sexy and had the nostalgic look of an old rigid frame, or hard tail, and looked like it was going fast even sitting still. The FXR and its fancier sister, the Low Rider, were enough like the predecessor FX bikes that very little had to be done for retooling. The Softails were simply a natural mate for the sleek Corbin Gunfighter seats. The Gunfighter seats became the most popular seat for the Softail and the FXR and were selling in unbelievable numbers. Later in the 80s, the Gunfighter seats were further spiffed up with the addition of flames of various colors as part of the trim.

Once again, Mike came up with a Harley seat idea at a rally, but this time at Sturgis, South Dakota. He was at the 1984 rally, and while leaning against his truck, taking a break; he began watching the huge numbers of new Softails going by. The Softail was a raging hit for Harley-Davidson. The bike looked like a rigid frame, and had a soft suspension, but the riders all looked uncomfortable.

The stock seats were convex and the rider couldn't really sit into the bike. It crowded the tail-bone and caused the rider to have to lean back too far with nothing to lean against, causing the effect of pulling for-

Softail with Gunfighter seat

ward with the stomach muscles and arms. This condition actually causes a greater pressure on the spine and tailbone. All of the riders on stock seats appeared to Mike to be riding by with sore backs.

Mike decided that he would create a seat that would solve the problem, by making one with two buckets, and have a removable backrest for the driver. Everyone he mentioned this idea to laughed at the concept. Undaunted Mike went back to Watsonville and began to work on this unique seat. He had invented a removable backrest back in the 70s, but had not patented it and had never perfected the concept. This time it was going to be great. The seat was born as the 161 Sturgis, which meant it was for Softail bikes and conceived at Sturgis. The 161 seat worked out well in both de-sign and sales. Custom Chrome picked up this new seat right away and they began selling like hotcakes. He had already developed a removable backrest for passengers that were great selling items and now there was a seat with backrests for both driver and passenger that didn't interfere with either and they were removable for more of a sporty look. The seat's official advertised name was the Canyon Dual Sport Seat and also known as the Gunfighter and Lady. This seat was available in both Softail and FXR configurations and with or without the backrest option. It was comfortable, solved the ergonomic problems, and best of all it looked and sold great.

In 1985, the company really started to grow with the popularity of the Gunfighter line of seats. The phenomenal sales of these seats built the company's name success of Corbin Pacific, Inc. Though unaware of it at the time, the hiring of two local youngsters to work on the Gunfighter seats, Cher Rosser and Vince Zavala, would become very fortuitous for the company. These two were destined to become two of the longest tenured, and most valued associates at Corbin Pacific, Inc. Ultimately, they would become like family and second only to Tom and Bev in the affection felt by Mike for those who are close to him.

By 1987, Mike had added the Rumble Seat to his growing collection of great selling ideas. This item was a flip-up back rest which would allow the seat to look like a normal Gunfighter seat when folded down and then flip up when a passenger seat was needed. In time, the Gunfighter Line of seats would be available for installation on all popular brands of motorcycles.

As the eighties were nearing the end of the decade, there was a lot to reflect on looking back. Mike had made a very hard decision to leave quite a bit of success, and a life he had known, to move three thousand miles and start all over. This would

Softail with rumble seat

be a very hard decision for anyone, even under the best circumstances. He made his decision and stuck it out, taking the cards where they fell, and as luck would have it, they all fell as aces. In seven years, Mike and his new company had once again achieved an unprecedented level of success. A huge success by anyone's standards, and all built around six new inventions. Those inventions were all conceived from Mike being at the right place at the right time and having the vision to see what was not already there. To paraphrase George Bernard Shaw, Mike sees things that are not yet here, and asks why not? He then sets about to create them.

1987 was also the year that Mike tried his hand at taking over Tennessee Williams' job as a playwright. Well, if not playwright, then perhaps screen writer. Mike wrote a movie script titled *Thunder & Lightning*. The story was about a motorcycle racer and written with National class drag racer, Dale Walker, as technical advisor. Had it been filmed, Dale would have played a part in the movie and also functioned as the film's technical advisor. Articles at the time touted the movie script as an exciting Saturday night adventure film that promises to elevate and excite bikers everywhere. Mike is still willing to speak with anyone about his screen writing debut and this potential film project.

The Earth seemed to be turning perfectly in its orbit, with life exactly as it should be for Corbin, and his new world, when disaster struck. It happened on an unusually warm and beautiful February afternoon, as Mike was accelerating onto Interstate Highway 280 South, headed back to Watsonville. A car, driven by a mentally disturbed person who had gone off his medicine, struck Mike and the red BMW K100RT motorcycle he was riding, pushing them into the Armco guardrail. The man in the car was supposed to be on medication for his mental disorder, which was not the

case. The police, it turned out, were already looking for the car involved due to an earlier assault
that same day. When the driver saw the red bike,
he immediately became paranoid and crossed the
four-lane freeway in order to strike Mike with the
car.

Mike had begun to accelerate to the speed
limit, but was climbing to speed slower than normal in order to remove his gloves. As warm as this
day was, he wanted to feel the wind on his hands.
Mike was unaware that he was being hit, only that
suddenly, he and the bike were accelerating much
faster than expected as the car struck the rear of
the bike.

As the bike hit the guardrail, Mike was
knocked off, and the car ran over his left side
breaking eighteen bones, including his ankles, left
arm and shoulder. The force of the impact stopped
his heart.

The first paramedics on the scene were
forced to kick Mike in the chest in order to restart
his heart, breaking five ribs in the process. Mike
never figured out if all five ribs were actually broken by the paramedics or by the accident itself.
Mike spent a long time in the hospital recovering
from the accident. It would be days before Mike
would be out of intensive care and no longer in
need of life support machines. There would be

many more days before he would return to a normal life. One reminder of the incident is a metal plate Mike carries in his shoulder, which serves as a troublesome source of annoyance for airport security guards.

Later, it was discovered that Mike was the third victim of this manic-depressive driver. The others were a woman with a shopping cart who was chased by this man in his car, and a child, who's back was broken when he rammed the car in which the child was riding. The driver fled the scene of the accident and was followed by a witness to a bar where he began bragging about killing a biker. The man's comments prompted the bartender to call the police. During his arrest he assaulted a policeman with a barstool. They arrested him only to find that there were two other outstanding warrants for his arrest. When questioned, he shrugged his shoulders and stated that he thought bikers sometimes had guns and could be dangerous. In his disturbed mind, the assault was a pre-emptive strike.

By late 1988,the little company that could, was making plans to vacate the Watsonville building. No longer the start-up it had been eight years earlier, they had out grown the building and Mike was planning to buy a vacant lot in Castroville and move the company into new digs. The purchase was made in 1989, and ground was broken for Corbin Pacific, Inc.'s first brand new building. There was one more thing they managed to find time to do; Mike and Bev were married on New Years Eve 1988, in a double wedding with their friends Mel Watts and his fiancée, Corrin.

Mike and Bev at the construction site in Castroville

Chapter 9
From Castroville To Dreams Fulfilled

When someone is lying in a hospital bed and wondering about things like, "Will I ever ride again," it's hard to imagine the future. But imagine Mike did and he still dared to dream. In fact, Mike has been a dreamer all of his life. As a child, he continuously dreamed that he would become an automaker. Some of his farthest back recollections are of walking home from school at age eight, he would imagine as he walked that he would make a car when he grew up. His father used to tell him he was crazy to think on that kind of scale. The dream came close in the seventies with the electric motorcycles and the car conversions, but not quite a dream realized.

Mike continued to dream all through the eighties and formulated a concept that Charlie MacArthur remembers as coming from the dairy product pouches in restaurants. These pouches usually contain something like creamer or sour cream and are wide at one end and very narrow on the opposite end. A vehicle built this way would have to be a three-wheeled configuration. Mike combined this concept with the attributes of a motorcycle. This was a dream he was determined to realize, but in 1988 there were other bridges to cross and roads to travel.

Mike began building in 1989, but it wasn't cars it was buildings in which to build seats and other motorcycle accessories. The company had purchased a vacant lot in Castroville and began construction of the first company owned new building. He now had forty employees, and business was beginning to grow even bigger than it had been. Seat orders were increasing daily as the economy recovered from the recessionary times of the previous decade. In short, Corbin Pacific, Inc. simply needed a bigger place to operate.

Corbin had already realized the Watsonville building was fast being outgrown and he had been negotiating for a bank loan when he was involved in the accident, but the banker thinking Mike might not survive or if he did, might be an invalid, had cancelled the negotiations. Mike did recover, of course, and business eventually returned to normal. The term normal is a relative one in the life of Mike Corbin. He actually began coming back into the plant earlier than the doctors felt he should have. Mike, being the iron-willed, hands-on, person he is, prevailed and rather than vegetate he began to come in to work.

With things back to business as usual, or as much so as possible in Mike's world, it was time to get back to the business of building a new place to put the business. Mike and Bev put up the equity in his condo as a down payment, and they began to plan a building to be the new home for the seat business. The new building in the Castroville location was constructed in 1989 and by the end of the year, Corbin Pacific, Inc. moved into its new digs at 11445 Commercial Parkway in Castroville.

Business continued to grow and Mike designed more and more things and delved deeper into the world of plastics and fiberglass. There were over two hundred seat offerings from Corbin by December of 1989 as reported by Cycle Magazine in a product evaluation test. Corbin had reclaimed the dominant place in the industry and once again commanded the number one market share position.

The year 1990 saw Corbin expand beyond seats in his quest for new endeavors in the motorcycle industry. Projects, which had little to do with seats, came along. In a cooperative effort, Corbin's fiberglass shop built the streamlined body for the Barnett / Kal-Guard "Project 200" sidecar attempt at breaking the 200 mph barrier for motorcycles with side cars. Although mechanical problems plagued the attempt, it did set a class record of 163.691. The machine, which conjures up images more akin to a flying saucer than resembling a motorcycle, actually achieved 174.636, giving it the distinction of being the fastest motorcycle with a sidecar in the world.

Mike Taylor of Barnett brought the project to Mike because he had heard of Mike's interest in fiberglass projects and knew of his outstanding work with motorcycle seats. Taylor remembers his first visit to Corbin. There was a truckload of the exercise machines being unloaded and he thought, "What else in the world can this guy possibly be into."

During the 1990 year, the Corbin Company, not only worked on its part of the sidecar project, but also managed to squeeze in the time to make and sell over 50,000 motorcycle seats.

Expansion did not stop with a new building. New ideas need new room to develop and more space to house them. By the summer of 1991, the still-new building again saw the presence of heavy equipment and construction. If the country was in a slow economic state, as reported, you couldn't find it in Castroville. Corbin Pacific added a 7200-ft^2 addition to the backside of the building. Tongue-in-cheek comments about Mike having a crane in his backyard abounded in the regional press. The project, which expanded the building, also housed a state-of-the-art vapor and dust removal system. In Mike's opinion, the most important thing they do is take care of the workers, which he refers to as associates. The company prides itself on an enviable safety record and an attitude of care for the employees.

In addition to the space needed for production, there was another motive and method in the madness. The intent to fulfill his childhood dream, and the desire make it a marriage with his dedication to environmental concerns. He needed to ultimately grow into having a facility with the infrastructure and skilled people to build that car – and make it run on electricity. The wheels in "Electric Mike's" head never stop turning as fast as the ones on whatever motorcycle he happens to be riding at any given time.

1991 was a year for other things to do, as if there wasn't enough to keep the crew busy. Children's charity events and benefits, as well as the inevitable motorcycle rallies were always present. The rally at Laconia, New Hampshire, found Mike back in the northeast showing off his creative handiwork with a French-made sidecar attached to a Yamaha FJ 1200 and sporting a custom Corbin interior.

Not all of the leather at Corbin Pacific was on saddles for bikes. While tush cushions were the mainstay of the business, other parts of the body were not left in the dirt, so to speak. Corbin offered a new line of comfortable and protective footwear with the line of Roadmaster riding boots. It was beginning to look as if the only thing you couldn't get at Corbin to make your riding experience more pleasurable was a massage after the ride. Then again, Mike's attitude was that if you were riding on one of his seats you wouldn't need the massage afterward.

Mike was possessed with a drive, not only to be successful, but to stay there as well. He had been a great admirer of George Smith, who founded S&S Cycle and Charlie Barnett, both of whom had built businesses from the ground up and whose businesses had not only succeeded, but had remained as pillars of the industry. Mike wanted, and wants to see his business to be around fifty years and longer. He has always wanted to build something that would have the longevity of a Hewlett-Packard or Beretta. He has tried to make his company a place where inventions thrive and has customers in need of the products produced.

To this end, he has given a green light to innovation and imagination on the part of his employees and promotes within the company when, and wherever possible. Mike needed good and skilled people who would be loyal and stay with the company if he were ever to realize his dreams of the future. For that goal he made the company a good place to work and one that would strive to keep the people who work there happy with their jobs. Mike once commented, "Whenever one of my people buys a new house, it makes me proud to know that the system is working."

He continued to stay deeply involved in the creation of new seats for each new model motorcycle presented to the public. The seat style inventory was growing, as was the business. The charity events were becoming more frequent, and Corbin's participation was increasing. One memorable ride was the transporting of Ronald McDonald around Laguna Seca Racetrack. Corbin was beginning to establish a reputation for being the first one to step up to the plate when it came time to dig for charity and especially if the charity was for children.

The Castroville location was working out wonderfully, and the seats were increasing in sales exponentially. In a 1993 interview, company marketing director, Greg Hurley, reported that the company had about 400 seat designs representing 200 different bikes and was shipping 150 seats daily, six days per week. Hurley also reported that the company had added a wide range of exotic styles of leathers, such as ostrich and alligator.

The fiberglass molding and modeling division was increasingly expanding the techniques and skills the company could produce and were being asked to create some very exotic designs.

Corbin teamed with Vance Breeze, owner of Santa Maria Harley-Davidson, in his effort to break the 300 plus mph barrier in a nitro burning, cigar shaped, and all-out speed machine, called the Santa Maria H-D Streamliner, nicknamed Mariah. The bike, which is designed to run at Bonneville, is 15 feet long, 25 inches high, and a mere 20 inches wide. A Harley-Davidson Sportster engine powers the machine. Corbin and his staff, which by now are building quite a reputation, were building the super strong and super light body from four hand molded layers of Kevlar.

The Streamliner was not the only such project bike the Corbin crew was working on in 1993. They answered the challenge to build a land speed bike body for Carl's Speed Shop, which at that time was still based on the West Coast.

This bike was, for Corbin, a beginning of the way of things to come, which added to, but drastically departed from seats. The Carl's Speed Shop bodywork was the prototype of what would become the Corbin Warbird series of motorcycle bodywork kits.

The year would also see the guys at Corbin, now being referred to as wizards, building the world's largest and sexiest Gunfighter seat. King Vini with Ultra Limo of Southern California, who was building a limo to resemble a giant Harley, contracted them to construct the seat. This was to be the most comfortable seat in the history of motorcycles. The giant seat was actually a hot tub. This was a seat you could really sit into. King Vini has since changed his name to "Big Daddy".

By 1993, Corbin Pacific had a new European division, and the dealer support mechanism was delivered a new van and its first stock of seats to their base at Antwerp.

Corbin Pacific set a new precedent in the motorcycle industry with the opening of a new permanent retail outlet at 504 Main Street in Daytona. No other manufacturer in the industry had ever taken such bold steps to reach the buying market. Daytona had been fertile ground for Corbin over the years, and as the company advertised and marketed at rallies through the 80s, and now 90s, they discovered that Daytona produced the largest percentage of sales of any single location, and in fact was responsible for roughly 50% of sales for all events attended. The new facility would not manufacture seats and accessories, but rather instead, would serve as Corbin's Bike Week and Biketoberfest headquarters for seat sales, and for the rest of the year, it would be the hub and warehouse to support the Eastern US and European distribution, as well as retail sales. Mike issued a statement with the announcement of the store opening that it would not be in competition with any existing Corbin dealers.

As if 1993 didn't have enough to crow about already, there is still more to say about it. The company was having a banner year in seat sales, and Mike was celebrating twenty-five years of designing, inventing, and marketing better ways to sit on a motorcycle. As if firsts were becoming a routine event for Corbin, to celebrate the 25th anniversary achievement, the company presented to the two-wheeled buying public a catalog unlike any other. Touted as a seat encyclopedia, this catalog featured sixteen full color pages showcasing dramatic designs and a section on styles and application information one hundred and forty four pages in length. All this to offer motorcycling an unheard of line of saddles numbering over two hundred, and fitting more than one hundred and ten bike models. This unique book of iron horse saddlery included additional products ranging from Corbin accessories to top of the line products by other manufacturers of interest to bikers. Sales were going great and prosperity had settled in on Mike and his seat company in a way unmatched in the industry. Happy anniversary Mike.

On a sad note, 1993 would also be the year that Mike's mother, Mary, passed away from Alzheimer's disease at 80 years of age. Her last years had been spent periodically living with Mike and Bev.

1994 came roaring in with a battle cry; the battle cry of a Warbird that is. The development lessons gleaned from designing and building the wind cutting body work and air diversion front fender for the Carl's Speed Shop Bonneville bike, led to the creation of Corbin's Warbird.

Hailed as the "Master Of The Wind", the Warbird was a sleek and beautiful kit for customizing Harley-Davidson's Sportster and the FXR models. Easy to assemble, these kits made it possible for a bike owner at almost any level of expertise to create a work of art, and the degree of performance was dependant only on the depth of the owner's pocket. With custom paint and some chrome spiffs, a bike outfitted in a Warbird configuration looked for all the world like an eagle cutting the air after prey. Even sitting still, these bikes looked fast.

Carl's Speed Shop was one of the first to utilize a Warbird for show and speed. Ridden by Doug Morrow, Carl's champion drag racing son, the custom orange painted Warbird was a ground pounding war eagle on the road or track. The famed motorcycle artist, Eric Herrmann, painted this unusual bike with Doug at the helm taking off like an F-4 Phantom Jet from an aircraft carrier. This depiction of the Warbird might have been unknowingly an eerie flash into the past, or a foretelling of the future, or both, in as much as the early experiments with electric motorcycles and cars were powered with starter motor / generators from F-4 Phantoms, and the development of the Warbird was the link to the future and a return to electric transportation. Maybe the spirit in the machine was somehow speaking to Eric subliminally.

The 1994-year was otherwise pretty uneventful as years go, if rising prosperity can be termed uneventful. Warbirds were selling and so were seats at phenomenal rates. Mike continued to contribute to children's charities for which he received a letter of commendation for his efforts from the Pediatric Brain Tumor Foundation's Ride For Kids.

He began to be regarded, in some circles, as someone to consult about design and marketability. By December 1994, Mike had received a letter of gratitude from the Research and Development Department of Honda of North America for his assistance and consultation. Joe Boyd, Senior Engineer of Motorcycle Engineering Research, wrote, "Your input and insight regarding the GL market is extremely helpful to our ongoing product planning and development efforts."

With a very prosperous several years behind him, Mike entered the new year 1995 with enthusiasm. Almost everything was working as it should, and his company was succeeding the way he had imagined it would when he set out to begin over in the early eighties. The saddles had reached the level of being a status symbol in motorcycling. Bikes sporting a Corbin Saddle automatically increased in value. Warbird kits were literally flying out the door, and with the success of the Warbird, another milestone had been reached. Perfecting the Warbird concept meant that his Workshop of Wizards, as his design shop and staff were now being called, was finally ready to tackle more complex shapes and molding in plastics and fiberglass. One item of particular interest to Corbin and his now capable crew was the compound curves involved in the shapes of things like fiberglass saddlebags.

These presented a particular problem because of the difficulty in removing them from the molds after they were cast or laid up, as it were. It is relatively easy to make wet fibers and resin conform to any surface shape, regardless of the complexity. Removing the piece after it has set up is quite a different situation entirely. Seat pans, Warbird parts, and saddlebags were only a fraction of the conglomerate of items the idea guys were concocting. Nose cones would eventually pave the way to fairings, which improve the aerodynamics of the bike, and couches styled after classic car trunks. None of these were the goal Mike had in mind; however, his end result was to be the fulfillment of his life long dream.

He began to discuss his dream idea with Vince Zavala, the head of the Research and Development department. This was the same young man who had begun working at Corbin right out of high school, mixing foam by hand to pour in seat molds. Now, ten years later, Vince had progressed to the skill level of master model maker. It would be possible, now that the business was stable and financially sound enough, to plan on returning to his roots and creating electric solo transportation. Mike began making some preliminary drawings depicting how he felt a simple electric car should look. He shared his ideas with Vince to get his artistic input, and they started to work together on the concept and design.

There were other plans in the works for Corbin Pacific that would put the little car creation temporarily on the back burner. The company had outgrown the store in Daytona. Corbin Pacific had grown to 80% of the market share in aftermarket seats. The current retail and distribution store at 504 Main was simply too small for the unbridled growth of the company, and it needed a larger facility. Mike solved the problem by purchasing a 38,000 Ft^2, warehouse building at 777 Main. The new facility was across the street and just two blocks down from the old location. They began to have extensive restoration and cosmetic remodeling done to the building, with an estimated target completion date planned for summer, 1996. Part of the plan was to have a beautiful showroom complete with hardwood floor, a display stage, and turntable to showcase the latest creation at each event.

Near the end of the year, Sonny Barger, the then president of the Oakland Hells Angels, approached Mike. Sonny knew that the 50th anniversary of the 1947 Hollister, California rally would be in 1997, just a little over a year away. Sonny felt that this was such a historic event for motorcycling that it would be a shame for it to pass without a commemorative event. He asked Mike to help plan something, and intercede with the town officials to make it happen. Mike had a special place in his heart for this event because it, or rather the movie about it, had been his early inspiration. He agreed that an event needed to happen, so answering to his heart, he said OK. It turned out that his heart was going to reach deep into his pocketbook.

After the 1995 Sturgis, South Dakota event, Mike returned to Castroville to get things in order so he could leave for Europe to straighten out the distribution over there. There were some problems that couldn't be handled long distance. A short time before leaving, Mike's son, Tom and his wife, Jennifer, came down from Sacramento to meet with Mike for lunch. During the meal, Mike was telling Tom about his upcoming trip and his plans for the future. He told Tom that things were going extremely well with the company. They were doing six times as much business as they had been doing in 1989 and were up to a production level of 200 seats per day. The previous March, a five-week month, they had produced over a million dollars in saddles. The company was stable and had five people in the European office, six in Daytona, and 87 in Castroville. He said he was to a point in his life where, now in his 50s, he was at an age where he was thinking about doing something really different. He said he was ready to begin pursuing his lifelong dream. He said, "I don't really want to sell my company, and I don't have anybody who can take it over." He said, My Company is now strong enough that I might be able to work on my car."

Tom had been going his own way since high school and really had little interest in being in motorcycling. He wanted to make his life a success rather than ride on his dad's success. He started out selling vacuum cleaners, then real estate, and finally became a real estate developer. Tom was between developments, but was preparing to start another one and build back up his real estate assets again. The two then had the most fateful dialog of their lives.

When Mike told Tom about his plans and mentioned working on the car, Tom said, "You might be able to work on the car?"

Mike said, "Yeah."

Then Tom replied, "Well then Dad, I don't have that many commitments now. I'm just getting ready to build my real estate assets back up, but I don't have any commitments." He said, "If you're going to do the car, I'm in with you – I mean I'm there."

Mike said, "That would be fabulous. Well, I am going to need someone to help me run the motorcycle seat company while I am inventing the car, and also, someone to help line up all the car stuff and figure it out."

Tom said, "Great! Well, the worst case scenario is if we try it and it doesn't work - right - work on it for one year, or two years, or three years, or however much time we feel we need to commit to it. I can either stay in the motorcycle seat business with you, or I can go back into real estate. I can do that at any time because I know how to do real estate. I don't think we have anything to lose, and why let a dream die with you or go to the grave with you."

Mike said, "That's right."

Mike had to go to Europe on the aforementioned trip to deal with a bad master distributor who was causing things to be messed up over there. They agreed that Tom would go with him, and while there, they would spend the time, day and night, talking it out. They would discuss what the dream was and what the idea was and how they were going to build the car.

They agreed that Tom would start January 2, 1996, as Executive Vice President at Castroville, helping with the company and helping with the car. Mike had his first California employee back with him, and was on the way to making the dream he had carried with him all of his life a reality. Or was he?

Chapter 10
Fly Sparrow Fly

Mike and Tom were finally working together again as a team for the first time since Tom had worked there as an after school and summer job. He wasted no time getting into the company and using the skills he brought on board with him. There were things in Tom's repertoire that were assets to the company, which had been short suits prior to his coming on board. He was experienced in many things that had not ever been issues in making seats, but which would become issues with getting a motor vehicle off the ground; things like permits, state and federal government regulations, and complex contracts.

The overall plan was to ramp up into production on a fairly grand scale; therefore, money circumstances were an issue. Of prime importance were things such as locating investors and handling their investments. These were areas of expertise in Tom's background. Plans were being made to begin the car project, and Tom would be spearheading the business end of it.

While the car project was incubating and preliminaries were being put into place, there was the little matter of a 50th anniversary Hollister motorcycle event.

Much of the event planning fell on Tom's shoulders and particularly the logistics of the event, and Mike, Tom, and Sonny decided to try a preliminary small rally in 1996 to check out the response. With Mike spearheading the event, Tom doing the legwork, and Sonny's influence, the event was on and the test one went smoothly. No real problems, at least no more than any new event, although this one was 49 years old.

In the meantime, while running around the California countryside doing rally stuff, Tom was still working with his dad to create the electric car. A car that would license as a motorcycle.

The Corbin team took the project from sketches to a tubular steel prototype that ran. With the prosperity that the saddle company was enjoying, it was able to take on additional manpower and funnel off enough talent and labor to make the car project happen. One of the former employees at the time, John Ortiz, remembers Mike ordering a 4' x 8' piece of plywood placed on the floor and saying to the crew, "We are going to build a car and it has to fit within the perimeter of that piece of plywood."

It was decided to once again name the product being created after a bird. Mike and Bev are very fond of birds and at the time had two African Gray parrots. One named Dirty Mike and his com-

panion, Sarah. Unlike the Warbird, or some other such name depicting a bird of prey, this item was to be called Sparrow. This car would not go thundering over the road, rather

John Ortiz testing the Sparrow prototype

slip quietly along carrying commuters quickly in and out of metropolitan areas.

Just as he had been with Bobbie Gentry and the *Ode To Billy Joe*, twenty-six years earlier, Mike was inspired again to choose a name from a Country & Western song by a female vocalist. This time from the Tanya Tucker song, *Two Sparrows In A Hurricane*.

Mike liked the song and reasoned that sparrows are everywhere and are a simple little bird that does no harm to anyone, and adapts well to its location and circumstances. He planned for his little car to be just that way also.

Once they were past the test Hollister event, they worked at a fever pitch to have a real prototype ready for the November San Francisco Auto Show as the first debut for the new vehicle. All this was going on while development of seats and accessories still had to go on and on schedule. This time, the Wizards in the workshop, were really doing some magic to make everything come in on time. Biketoberfest at Daytona came and went and it was show time.

The first car was ready to unveil, and this time it really resembled a bird. Tweety Bird. The Sparrow was a bright canary yellow and egg shaped with two wheels in front and a single drive wheel in the rear. Sure enough, it had a motorcycle type drive and qualified under California and federal law as a motorcycle. This time, a motorcycle that the rider sat in, rather than on.

Mike says he was scared to death. He was afraid that he would be laughed out of the show. Much the same way he had feared the worst after the first five seats were delivered to Sal Scirpo. November 18th press releases were sent out and the car made its grand entrance in the "City by the Bay", on November 24th.

The fears were ill founded, and the little car

was the hit of the show. Mike and Tom returned home ecstatic and determined more than ever to make a success of Mike's dream. The father and son team may not have been flying like birds, but they were surely walking on air all the way back to Castroville.

The seat company is still growing during this time although somewhat ignored by Mike. Mike had Vince working on the Sparrow project, while he divided his

The Sparrow - unveiled

own time between the two. Mike was still developing seats for the newest model bikes and related accessories but the Sparrow was his passion during that time. Tom, meanwhile, was working on the logistics of bringing to fruition the Hollister event for Mike and Sonny.

Mike, along with Barnett Tool and Engineering, Performance Machine, and Carl's Speed shop had for the previous couple of years, hosted a party and dinner at the Sturgis event for the media. This dinner was used to show off the companies' respective latest offerings and schmooze with the press. Usually, this press party would result in articles being written to test or at least alert the motorcycle public what was new in the industry. Mike chose the 1996 party to inform the press of his planned Hollister event and tell of the new car project.

Tom Corbin had originally feared that he and his dad might conflict, but this was not to be the case. Mike is the chief designer and dislikes the little details of running a business. This had caused some of the conflicts when he was with Corbin-Gentry. He would later come to learn that he had to pay attention to the little details of his business. Tom, on the other hand, loved the intricate details of business and therefore was the perfect counterpart to Mike. Any fears of a Corbin conflict were not to be realized. The two made a good team and loved working together, each somewhat autonomously doing his respective job. Tom does freely admit, however, that at the end of the day he still calls Mike, Chief, and the power comes from the top.

The various projects were eating resources at a rapid clip, but the seat company seemed to be holding its own financially and generating enough revenue to pay all of the expenses.

The lessons learned on building Warbirds, as well as the land speed machine bodies for other would-be record breakers, paved the way for the construction of the Sparrow. The safety of this type of construction was inadvertently proved when Vance Breeze crashed his similarly constructed Streamliner named, Mariah, and survived because of this type of construction.

The shell of the Sparrow was a sandwich, much the same as a surfboard, with an ovaloid, or roughly egg shaped design. This is one of the strongest structures known to exist. Sparrows involved in accidents provided such good protection that the drivers emerged virtually unhurt.

With the extra people hired for the Sparrow project, the employment level at Corbin reached 137, and the car project began to take more and more resources from the seat manufacturing. At the time, this was not as apparent as it should have been. A situation that would come to be very destructive for the idea guy.

In the mean time, things were progressing with the plans for the Hollister rally, as well as the opening of the new facility in Daytona. The new East Coast, 38,000 Ft^2, headquarters for Corbin, nicknamed the Taj Mahal, was a real show place. Easily, the most elaborate building on Daytona's famed Main Street, the two-story art deco building had come into service only after an enormous amount of renovation was performed to make it a suitable for the Corbin purpose. Between the seats, the car, the new building, and the rally, 1996 was, perhaps, the busiest year ever in the history of Corbin Pacific.

Tom was spending his time raising capital for the car project and doing the legwork for the rally. Sonny and Mike believed that California needed a large rally; the magnitude of a Daytona or Sturgis. They were convinced that it was possible and necessary. After all, Hollister was considered the birthplace of the American Biker, or at least the image, as we know it. This event would be a way of giving back to the industry. The enthusiasm was infectious and people from all over the US began planning to attend. Mike and Tom were both caught up in this enthusiasm and proceeded with all speed to pull it off.

Along with seats, the Warbirds were going great guns and even Mike Taylor of Barnett, constructed a custom Warbird from an old tired FXR he owned. Between the advertising that was already being done and the real show stoppers of Carl's, and Barnett; the Warbird became a major seller in the motorcycle accessories business. Sales across the board were staying up and climbing, making funding the car project relatively easy to justify. In 1995, the company had done exceptionally well in sales, and there was the promise of 1996 becoming an even greater year for the company. There was just too much going on to keep track of all of the details, which was Mike's least favorite part of being in a successful business.

October and Biketoberfest was the setting for the grand opening of the new Daytona facility, and the motorcycle industry was able to see accessory sales presented in a level of grandeur unheard of prior to this time. The Corbin Grand Opening was a great party and would be repeated annually for several years thereafter.

The Hollister rally was something else entirely. Tom's efforts were paying off, at least as far as results were concerned. Some eighty acres near the airport was leased for the rally site, and the town came online with a general attitude of support. The younger Corbin put together a grand event. At the rally site was a large compound for vendors and their large trucks. A large amphitheatre was erected, and among the entertainment was a band composed of former members, and some front people originally in other top bands, doing the latest incarnation of Creedence Clearwater Revival.

Downtown things were equally hot, and everyone's favorite place to be was at the café and bar made famous in Stanley Kramer's film, The Wild One, with Lee Marvin and Marlon Brando.

The event had a huge fenced in area, camping areas, paramedics, emergency services, and a helicopter in the event anyone needed to be medevaced out.

As rallies go, it was a success and attracted about fifty thousand participants. The town expected, or more accurately feared, that attendees would number in excess of 150,000, and the city officials effectively forced Corbin to have facilities for that many. The original Hollister rally, in 1947, wasn't the riot the media and the movies portrayed it to be either. Just nine days after the event, the town was planning another motorcycle meet for the same year. On a side note it was calculated that the 1947 event generated about $50,000.00 in revenue for the town and its merchants.

This event has grown since 1997, to over a hundred thousand participants annually. The costs for the 50th anniversary event were borne by Corbin almost exclusively, without the profits, and were in excess of $600,000.00.

There were some inevitable minor controversies in connection with planning the event. Tom was frustrated in his efforts to obtain the town's Bolado Park Fairgrounds as part of the event. Other promoters were trying to stage their own Hollister rally and had acquired the rental contract on the fairground first. A few unfortunate incidents occurred during the event, and at one point some youth gang members attempted to start some trouble downtown.

There is an old saying that if you need something done take it to the busiest character you know and have him do it for you. In all probability, no company, or family, in the motorcycle industry was busier than the Corbins and Corbin Pacific, and everyone kept coming to them to handle projects. Keeping your wits about you with this much activity and involvement builds character says Mike. Mike says, "We liked it, and we managed to pull it off."

They never did recover the funds spent on the 50th anniversary rally and Mike figures they never will. There would be no way to track it anyway. He simply has decided to chalk it up to good promotion and a major contribution to the motorcycle industry that he loves so much.

In spite of the rally losses and money spent on the car project, Corbin Pacific, Inc. expected 1997 to be a banner year in sales of seats and accessories.

Prior to the rally, Tom had arranged to ac-

Tom and Mike holding a 1997 Hollister poster

quire the land for Mike to build a new and larger facility in Hollister and move the company yet another time to keep up with the growth of the business and the industry.

They had agreed to purchase eleven acres across from the Hollister airport, near the site of the rally, and build a new 82-100,000 Ft² building. They were also arranging a tenant relationship with American Eagle Motorcycles.

The move to Hollister, along with American Eagle, would mean additional jobs and revenue for the town. Mike felt that by being in Hollister, with its heritage and history in motorcycling, would be a good move promotionally.

The seat business was still growing, but lurking in the woodwork was something as sinister and damaging as termites are to a house. The Corbin Company house was the victim of misinterpretation and unknowing neglect.

Where Mike was the inventor, as always, and a master at bringing production along to be ready by day of sale. He was woefully ill equipped to ride herd on all of the minute details of day-to-day nuts and bolts business.

The new building was completed late in 1997, and the company made its move to Hollister New Year 1998. It was after this point that the "termite effect" began to eat away at the foundation. Although the financial support was growing larger by leaps and bounds, it was countered by a financial erosion factor growing at an even faster rate than the income.

Moving into and setting up the new building was an astronomical expense, in both manpower as well as cash.

In addition to the building and the car, there were other projects taking resources and time away

After the move to Hollister

from the seat company, which was paying the freight for everything. There were custom couches, new fairings, molded hard saddlebags, and two Corbin sponsored Bonneville projects. One of these was an attempt at another speed record with a three-cylinder, triumph-powered bike, and the other was designed to demonstrate that the aerodynamics of the Corbin Saddlebags would keep the bags from creating excess friction, or a dam effect, thus, interfering with the airflow over the bike. This experiment was successful and resulted in the world's only 200 MPH saddlebags.

Although most would end up paying for themselves in the long haul, the research and development was costly for each project in both money and manpower. In business terminology this is called burn-rate. Burn-rate is the speed in which resources, all of which render down to costs in cash, are used up during the time to day-of-sale. This is analogous to an ambulance, in a life or death emergency, on a rural road, approaching a railroad crossing with no signal system, while simultaneously a long train is heading toward that same intersection. Ideally, the ambulance reaches the crossing, with a good margin, ahead of the train. If the train gets there first, then there is either a catastrophic crash or potentially a fatal delay. The time to day-of-sale must be less than the terminal velocity of the burn-rate.

In an effort to develop the Sparrow into a viable production vehicle, it spun off into a separate company, called Corbin Motors, and began occupying a separate manufacturing and operations location, from the seat company. This was during the Dot Com prosperity era, and there were many people who wanted to invest in the Sparrow, but Corbin Pacific was a wholly owned company and couldn't take in investors.

The newly formed company went immediately into the business of promoting the car and qualifying potential investors. The plight of the little car; however, was not in finding investors. People were almost standing in line to get in on the new vehicle concept of a personal transportation module, which simply means a commuter vehicle. The problem was the same as the barriers that Babbage encountered when he developed the first computer. The technology on the supply side had not kept up with the technology on the creation side. The ghost in the machine was that they were plagued with bad marriages of components. Almost all worked, but none of them were designed to work with each other, and like partners in any bad marriage, there were insurmountable conflicts. It was ultimately a solvable problem, but time was running out, the burn rate headed to zero, and the terminal time to return of investment was fast approaching.

The crash of the Dot Com was a turning point downward and suppliers reduced investing in efforts to get into production of workable components. The fall of the economy after the September 11, 2001 attack on the World Trade Center had investors and suppliers across the board running scared. Both money and parts slowed to a trickle.

In an effort to be into production with a viable vehicle for sale, while technology and supply was catching up in the electronics arena, the company produced an intermediate product that had fired the desire of ownership in almost everyone who saw it. This was the Merlin. In keeping with the Workshop Of Wizards motif, the name was apropos, and it could have worked the magic needed to be Corbin Motors' salvation. Orders were pouring in, and but for a little more time, positive cash flow would have happened with the Merlin. The Merlin began with a concept prototype coupe in 2000, and by May 2001, was developed as a Roadster. By August of 2001, a running version of the roadster made its debut at the Sturgis Motorcycle Rally.

There was a similar ghost in this machine also, and it haunted them like a malevolent poltergeist. The Merlin had been originally conceived to have a newly designed engine. This engine was to be produced by a company with which Corbin Motors had joined forces. The new engine had failed to meet necessary performance specifications to go into the roadster, and consequently, the Merlin was redesigned, to be powered by an existing Harley-Davidson type engine. Here now was the rub. The car mated well with the engine, but after a while the engine crankshafts would break. Many theories were tried to alleviate the problem and all worked for a while, then the cranks would inevitably fail. This problem was solved but the discovery of the solution came too late by a matter of days. Both companies were stretched to the limit. Corbin Pacific was investing every cent it could find into the Merlin, but there would not be enough there to wave the wizard's magic wand in time.

Another major problem was not mechanical, but in personnel. Mike had taken in management people to run the company and all had been successful executives elsewhere. The problem was an apple and orange one. Executives at higher corporate levels deal more in decision-making and company politics than being in the trenches with the troops. They are salary driven rather than the end result. Mike had inadvertently brought into his company, people in management on both the motor company side and the seat company side, who were on a different agenda than the project-focused mindset of Mike and Tom. For this misreading of intentions, Mike readily blames himself.

The father & son team are both driven by the creation of the product, and the goal of bringing it to market on time. Never being motivated by the end result in dollar signs, Mike is motivated, instead, by creating something unique, practical, and needed. He had worked hard with his seemingly endless drive, and the dollars just seemed to fall into place. His crew of wizards all followed suit. It simply didn't occur to Mike that every one would not follow that same mindset and work ethic.

Corbin came to the painful realization that there was a mismatch and finally would have to restructure. Among the ones to go were mem-

Mike's wife Beverly Corbin

bers of upper management, including the President, who was relieved of his position and replaced by Tom. Later, when things still could not be brought into sync, the former president, now vice president, was removed altogether. Unfortunately, he still held a great deal of stock and a large note against the motor company. When he was terminated, he was angry, and he wanted his investments returned with profits. He foreclosed on the

Mike Corbin

note and forced Corbin Motors into receivership.

In mid March 2003, Tom was forced to file for a Chapter 7 bankruptcy on behalf of Corbin Motors. This action took place on a Monday, and the following Friday the Sheriff arrived with orders to seize all of Corbin Motors' assets. All material assets were confiscated, even to the last wrenches and office pencils. With that action, the lifetime dream of the son of Irish immigrants, Walt and Mary; the little car that had shown so much promise and hope for the future and the environment — was no more.

Epilog

The Sparrow was conceived from a dream, which hatched and flexed its wings during the boom of the Dot-Com era. Money was being made and people saw this alternative little car as an answer to the dilemma of over crowded commuting lanes. An idea, not before its time, rather before the times were ready for it and technology able to provide support.

Everybody lost in its demise because foreclosure of a company is its death rattle. The investors, those who wanted the cars, and a world that needed the shining hope cradled in the wings of the Sparrow and Merlin's magic wand. The Sparrow was an icon. The icon which could have ushered in the paradigm shift needed in an over crowded society gradually choking off its mobility.

The last days of Corbin Motors were a nightmare for Mike and Tom Corbin. The days following were even worse, for this period was one of terrible depressive stress and loss for Mike. The production delays had been maddening enough, but the lack of capital affected survival itself. Tom was also devastated and his personal finances were completely exhausted. A little more funding and another thirty days and Corbin Motors might have survived

Mike Corbin was the inventor, the master at bringing products to market on time. Not unlike others before him, for all inventors are the ultimate optimists, he pursued his dream and became so focused on the car, that he did not see the seat company slipping away, and almost to the point of being lost itself. In the end he says, "It was all my fault. I did not know how to do the due diligence that was necessary."

In all probability, the man who foreclosed, even if he had a spiteful motive, coupled with his desire to recover his investment, thought that at the eleventh hour Mike would just reach into his deep pockets and pay off the note. If he did in fact believe this would happen, he didn't understand that the pockets now had holes in them, and were no longer deep. The seat company had been so drained of revenue that it was in a negative cash-flow situation. Mike was depleted of many personal resources and ultimately elected to sell off several properties in order to began recovery and satisfy creditors.

In the end, Mike's salvation came from unexpected sources. He had some aces that perhaps had been standing in the wings patiently waiting as the frantic spiral downward brought America's "Seat Ace", back to a hard landing.

The most notable one, being his partner in life. Bev Corbin is Mike's cheerleader and his rock of support. Mike is a doer and not a 9-5 person. His life is his dedication to his work and he has to pursue his dreams. Bev, above all, understands him. Tom has said, "Very few people have a spouse who will understand a work ethic like Mike's. If you take the work out of Mike, you would take his life away."

Another is his Workshop and the wizards who help him work the magic. Vince (Wiz), Cher, Julio, Rosa, Ignatio (Nacho), and Esther. All there since the Watsonville days, over twenty years, and others like Sandy, Greg, and Chance. The love and support of a loyal team that loves you and stays through the tough times as well as the great ones. As luck would have it, Mike had the good sense to see the coming of Target Market TV as an advertising medium and teamed with Dennis Gage in 2001, to produce Corbin's Ride On, the most popular motorcycle show on the Speed Channel.

And finally, the Harvard School of Business. At the outset of the Sparrow project, the concept of it, and Mike's business successes, attracted Harvard to do a case study on him. This association led to Mike's enrollment in a three-year, Owners Presidents & Managers course at Harvard, and subsequent graduation in 2002.

The demise of the little electric car forced Mike to draw upon the lessons learned at Harvard, and he put to work what he had learned. Once again, he had to reinvent himself and crawl back up, like the mythical phoenix from its ashes. An important lesson he has learned from life, as well as Harvard, is that even an inventor has to run his own business, even the nuts and bolts. You can not get someone else to do it.

He has learned that he could reinvent again and climb back from ruin. As of the writing of this book, Corbin Pacific, Inc. is again solvent. Mike will tell you, the would-be entrepreneur, that it's worth taking the risk.

I will tell you, the reader, to keep your eye on Corbin. The inventor, the risk taker, has come full circle, and is back in his basement shop, as he was when Robbie was born, and some new concept, with the spirit of the little sparrow and the heart of an eagle, will soon take flight.

Media Research Bibliography

AMERICAN BIG TWIN *Dec. 1993*
AMERICAN IRON MAGAZINE *Dec. 1994, May 2002*
AMERICAN MOTORCYCLE DEALER *Jan. 2004*
AMERICAN RIDER *Dec. 1996, June 2002, Aug. 2002, Nov./Dec. 2003 ,*
    Feb. 2004, July/Aug, 2004,
AUTO WEEK *Aug. 11, 1997*
AUTOMOTIVE EXECUTIVE *June 1997*
BARNETT'S *Dec./Jan.1999/2000*
BARNETT'S NATIONAL CYCLE SELLER *Nov./Dec.2000*
BIKE UND BUSINESS (GERMAN) *2004*
BIKER *Feb. 1996*
BMW OWNERS NEWS *July,2003*
CANADIAN BIKER *Nov. 2003*
CITY BIKE *March, 1992*
CYCLE NEWS *Aug. 20, 1997, June 13, 2001,*
CYCLE WORLD *1997*
CYCLE *Dec. 1989*
DEALER NEWS *June 1991, Sept.. 1996, Oct. 2000, July 2002*
EAGLE'S EYE *Dec. 1994*
EASY RIDER (GERMAN) *Jan. 1994*
EASY RIDERS *Dec. 1995*
EASY RIDERS V-TWIN *Nov.1993*
ELECTRIC VEHICLE PROGRESS *Dec. 15, 1996*
EUROPEAN DEALER NEWS *Sept..1993*
EVENING CITIZEN CENTRAL NH
FLORIDA BIKERS DIGEST *Dec. 1996*
FREE 2 WHEEL *July 1991, Dec. 1995, 1996, 1997*
FREE LANCE, Hollister, CA. *Feb. 23, 1996, May 1, 1997, Oct. 7, 2003*
FREEWAY (FRENCH) *1994, 1998, 2000,*
FULL THROTTLE *2000*
GEARHEAD GAZETTE *1995*
GOLDWING TOURING ASSOCIATION *Aug. 1991*
GOODGUYS GOODTIMES GAZETTE *2000*
HACK'D *Fall '90, Fall '97*
HARD TWIST MAGAZINE *1994*

HOT BIKE *Nov. 1987, Dec, 1992, March 1993, Dec. 1994, Dec. 2000, Jan. 2004*
HOT ROD BIKES *1997*
IRON WORKS/ IRON TRADER NEWS *1993, 1994, Dec. 1996*
KING OF THE ROAD *Jan. '97*
LA BIKE *1991, 1993*
MCM (GERMAN) *1996*
MDT *Nov./Dec. 2003*
MOTOR STREET CRUISER *Dec. 2000, April 2001*
MOTORCYCLE INDUSTRY MAGAZINE *1991, 1992*
MOTORCYCLE NEWS
MOTORCYCLE PRODUCT NEWS *Feb. 1993*
MOTORCYCLE SHOPPER *April 1994*
MOTORCYCLE STREET & STRIP *2000*
MOTORCYCLE TOUR & CRUISER *Sept. 1999*
PARTS MAGAZINE *May '98*
POWER SPORTS *2001, July 2, 2001,Sept. 2, 2001, April 2003, Sept..8, 2003, 2004, Jan.2004*
RALLY *2001*
RIDER *June 1991, Nov. 1991, 1993, July 1997, Dec. 2004*
SHOWCASE *Dec. 2000*
STREET RODDER *April 2000*
STURGIS RALLY NEWS *Summer 1999*
THE CORBIN TIMES DAILY NEWS
THE ENGINEER *March 2002*
THE MOTORCYCLIST'S POST *Jan./Feb. 1994, Dec. 2002*
THE NEW YORKER *Aug. 12, 2002*
THE PINNACLE *May 8, 1997, June 12, 1997, Aug. 28, 2003, July 1, 2004*
THE SOUTHERN CALIFORNIA MOTORCYCLE GUIDE *Spring 1991*
THUNDER ALLEY *Feb.'96*
VQ
V-TWIN *Jan. 1999, April 2003, Aug. 2003, Oct. 2003, Nov. 2004*
V-TWIN NEWS/ DEALER NEWS *July 2003, Aug. 2003, Nov. 2003*
WING WORLD *Oct. 1991, Aug 1997, 2000*
WOMAN RIDER *Winter 2003*

About the Author

William Graham Carrington was born in Durham, North Carolina in 1945. The son of a newspaperman, he was exposed to current events and travel which coupled with a heavy historical influence from his mother, directed and shaped his thoughts and mind set. Except for liking baseball, was not into sports, but rather spent most of his time reading and playing with electronics and Amateur Radio.

While still in high school, he began an early career in radio as an announcer and production person and went on to school for radio engineering after graduation. Following this he attended The Don Martin School of Radio & Television Arts & Sciences and then continued his career in radio as an announcer, engineer, and production person. This resulted in the writing of an enormous amount of ad copy and producing radio commercials. In the mid-70's, he began to evolve from radio into commercial photography where he also became interested in writing the copy and producing the pieces for which the photos were being taken.

In 1988, a return to school at the University of North Carolina at Chapel Hill, resulted in several professors encouraging him to continue his studies, consider writing, and to complete a degree in journalism. After graduation, course work was continued in corporate video production and script writing. Since 1992, he has written audio and video scripts and many articles published in national and regional magazines about travel, history, business, personality profiles, and motorcycling. In 1995, he traveled nationally writing event articles for the Harley Davidson Motor Company.

Carrington is the author of two books of poetry, one of patriotic and motorcycling poems, a narrative history of America's cowboy image and its relationship to the popularity of motorcycling, and the current Corbin biography. In the fall of 1999, he was nominated for a year 2000 Pulitzer Prize. Two more poetry books are in progress, and the research is underway for one historical and one travel book. He performs his poetry and historical programs periodically before live audiences.

A motorcyclist since 1964, he has ridden all forty-eight contiguous states, won two awards for long distance riding, and has been nominated for the Motorcycle Hall Of Fame.

Other Books By William G. Carrington:

Cowboys With Chrome Horses   *$14.95*
ISBN 1-888701-02-1

Tomorrow's Promise And Other Poems *$11.95*
1-888701-07-02

Tomorrow's Promise And Other Poems *$14.95*
Audio Book
1-888701-08-0

Give Me The Wind   *$9.95*
1-888701-10-2

Forthcoming Books:

Flight of the Raven
1-888701-37-4

One Heart Beyond Tomorrow
1-888701-01-3

One Heart Beyond Tomorrow
Audio Book
1-888701-09-9

A Candle In The Window
1-888701-11-0

The Other End Of Main Street
1-888701-18-8

The Cost Of Arrogance
1-888701-21-8

Pennyworth Press
Book And Product Order Form

Credit Card Orders: Not available as of this printing

Email: *books@pennyworthpress.com*
Information: *http://www.pennyworthpress.com*

Postal Orders: Pennyworth Press, POB 25176, Asheville, NC 28813

Please send the following books / products:

_____

_____

_____

Book orders should include ISBN: _____

☐ **Please add me to the mailing list for author book signings, public appearances, updates, and upcoming books.**

Company name:_____

Name:_____

Address:_____

City:_____ State:_____ Zip:_____-_____

Telephone: (___)_____ Fax: (___)_____

Email address: _____

Shipping:$3.50 + $1.00 first book & $1.00 each additional. NC addresses add 6% tax

Payment:
Cheque or Money Order To:

Pennyworth Press
POB 25176
Asheville, NC 28813

®

Pennyworth Press
Book And Product Order Form

Credit Card Orders: Not available as of this printing

Email: *books@pennyworthpress.com*
Information: *http://www.pennyworthpress.com*

Postal Orders: Pennyworth Press, POB 25176, Asheville, NC 28813

Please send the following books / products:

_____

_____

_____

Book orders should include ISBN: _____

☐ **Please add me to the mailing list for author book signings, public appearances, updates, and upcoming books.**

Company name:_____

Name:_____

Address:_____

City:_____ State:_____ Zip:_____-_____

Telephone: (___)_____ Fax: (___)_____

Email address: _____

Shipping:$3.50 + $1.00 first book & $1.00 each additional. NC addresses add 6% tax

Payment:
Cheque or Money Order To:

Pennyworth Press
POB 25176
Asheville, NC 28813